Postcolonial Homiletics?

Postcolonial Homiletics?

Exploring Consciousness, Centers, and Identity for Preaching

WESSEL WESSELS

Foreword by
CAS WEPENER

☙PICKWICK *Publications* • Eugene, Oregon

POSTCOLONIAL HOMILETICS?
Exploring Consciousness, Centers, and Identity for Preaching

Copyright © 2024 Wessel Wessels. All rights reserved. Except for brief quotations in critical publications or reviews, no part of this book may be reproduced in any manner without prior written permission from the publisher. Write: Permissions, Wipf and Stock Publishers, 199 W. 8th Ave., Suite 3, Eugene, OR 97401.

Pickwick Publications
An Imprint of Wipf and Stock Publishers
199 W. 8th Ave., Suite 3
Eugene, OR 97401

www.wipfandstock.com

PAPERBACK ISBN: 978-1-6667-3487-4
HARDCOVER ISBN: 978-1-6667-9134-1
EBOOK ISBN: 978-1-6667-9135-8

Cataloguing-in-Publication data:

Names: Wessels, Wessel, author. | Wepener, Cas, 1972–,foreword.

Title: Postcolonial homiletics? : exploring consciousness, centers, and identity for preaching / Wessel Wessels ; foreword by Cas Wepener.

Description: Eugene, OR : Pickwick Publications, 2024 | Includes bibliographical references.

Identifiers: ISBN 978-1-6667-3487-4 (paperback) | ISBN 978-1-6667-9134-1 (hardcover) | ISBN 978-1-6667-9135-8 (ebook)

Subjects: LCSH: Preaching.

Classification: BV4211.2 .W430 2024 (print) | BV4211.2 .W430 (ebook)

All Scripture quotations, unless otherwise indicated, are taken from the Holy Bible, New International Version®, NIV®. Copyright ©1973, 1978, 1984, 2011 by Biblica, Inc.™ Used by permission of Zondervan. All rights reserved worldwide. www.zondervan.comThe "NIV" and "New International Version" are trademarks registered in the United States Patent and Trademark Office by Biblica, Inc.™

The Holy Bible, English Standard Version (ESV) is adapted from the Revised Standard Version of the Bible, copyright Division of Christian Education of the National Council of the Churches of Christ in the U.S.A. All rights reserved.

To Zakkai and Joshua

Contents

Foreword ix

Acknowledgments xii

Introduction 1

1. Genealogical Comparison between Black Theology of Liberation (BTL) and Postcolonial Thought 15
2. Postcolonial Preaching? Contemplation on Postcolonial Thought and Homiletics 68
3. Postcolonial Liturgical Contemplation 91
4. Contemplating Postcolonial Hermeneutics 125
5. Some Concluding Thoughts 143

Bibliography 159

Foreword

RECENTLY DURING A CLASS discussion in a homiletics module in South Africa, one of the students pointed through a window to a church building of a historically white mainline church and asked: "is it possible to preach the Gospel from colonial pulpits?" I want to extend the student's question to the academic field of Homiletics and ask whether it should be permissible for a white academic from South Africa to write about postcolonial preaching. I ask as this is what Wessel Wessels did in this book. How Wessels went about his task and the content he presented are significant in answering this question.

What is presented in this text is not what Swiss homiletician Jean-Jacques von Allmen calls docetic preaching, or docetic homiletics, in other words preaching or reflection on preaching that by-passed the body of the preacher or homiletician. On the contrary, this is an academic text which filters through a very specific (white and male) body and brain in a particular South African context. Wessel Wessels consciously embedded himself in an extremely challenging post-1994 and postcolonial South African context, and his academic reflections are molded by reflexivity regarding his identity in this context. This makes the research reported in this book an example of a specific kind of noetic quest; it is an embodied reflexive quest that simultaneously engages theory and praxis and is, as such, akin to what preaching as a practice should entail.

On yet another epistemological level, Wessels did not only use sources that many readers of homiletics books would expect to find in this book (even though the usual homiletical suspects are not absent from the text) but also chose to dialogue with fellow Africans and specifically with Black Theology of Liberation. He combines Black Theology of Liberation with insights from Postcolonial Theory and critically scrutinizes developments in South African homiletics. As such, he is the first South African scholar to tend to this huge research gap in homiletics, and he does so in an auspicious and meaningful way.

Postcolonial Theory has influenced many disciplines, but only recently have homileticians begun to apply insights from Postcolonial Theory in homiletics. The legacy of colonialism is still discernible in places such as South Africa. In addition, preachers are often powerful role players who can challenge or perpetuate persistent oppressive systems. The potential to either challenge or perpetuate oppressive structures and death-dealing narratives is embedded in the whole homiletical process—from exegetical and hermeneutical approaches right through to how preaching is performed by preachers and appropriated by hearers, and even extends to how homiletical research is conducted. Employing the practice of postcolonial preaching, the possibility of interruption becomes possible. Dominant narratives are challenged, and alternatives are imagined. This aim of Postcolonial Homiletics is reminiscent of how Walter Brueggemann, in *The Prophetic Imagination*, described Moses' work as prophet: "an assault on the consciousness of empire, aiming at nothing less than the dismantling of the empire both in its social practices and its mythic pretensions!"[1]

To achieve this emancipatory task by means of preaching, Wessels sees much potential in the aesthetic approach to homiletics. This is a kind of preaching that aims at reimagining, reconfiguring, and reframing. In the words of Brueggemann regarding preaching, it is "an act of imagination, that is, an offer of an image through which perception, experience, and finally faith can be reorganized in alternative ways."[2] In this regard, Wessels provides a critical and appreciative engagement with the homiletical oeuvre of the South African homiletician Johan Cilliers.

Can Wessel Wessels' work help answer the student's question of whether it is possible to proclaim the gospel from colonial pulpits? *Postcolonial Preaching?* makes it clear that postcolonial preaching is a form of art, an art form that should be approached in a critical-reflexive mode and as a noetic quest that continuously and simultaneously makes use of multiple sources. Wessels' methodology, combined with his epistemology, shows that it is imperative, also, for white preachers to preach the gospel from colonial pulpits. However, when a preacher engages in the practice of postcolonial preaching, the student's question of whether it is indeed possible to do so should never be exhaustively answered. Much like the

---

1. Brueggemann, *Prophetic Imagination*, 9.
2. Brueggemann, *Word Militant*, 29.

Foreword

question mark in the title *Postcolonial Homiletics?*, the student's question should accompany preachers while they prepare their sermons and remain with them when they climb the steps into the pulpit.

Cas Wepener
Professor of homiletics, Stellenbosch University, South Africa

Acknowledgments

It astonished me how many people could influence one's thoughts throughout a project such as a PhD. I can hardly remember some of the influences in detail, yet I know their impacts have been profound. Many friends have been gained in this process, but the contentious nature of this topic might have located me outside of the spheres of others. It is to those who would continue an engaged discussion for whom I am most grateful—even under the circumstances or differences. Cas Wepener and Stephan de Beer, I appreciate your meticulous comments and direction on the first writings of this project. Colleagues at the Department of Practical and Missional Theology at the University of the Free State, where we have a weekly discussion group—especially to those who are most keen to dialogue, Martin Laubscher, Kobus Schoeman, and Jan-Albert van den Berg—you are exceptional theological sparring partners. To my friends and family, your support has kept me sane, and I am forever grateful.

Wessel Wessels
March 2023

Introduction

As far as I am aware, postcolonial insights have only been considered within homiletics in a handful of North and South American literature.[1] In South Africa, there has not been any homiletic work that has explicitly worked with postcolonial insights. Thus, postcolonial theory is an unexplored space within South African homiletics which should be engaged.

However, from the very onset of this engagement with postcolonial insights, I recognize that different meanings (often contested) are included under the postcolonial label. Even more, decolonization and decoloniality are used interchangeably with postcolonial. In my understanding, there is a consensus that decolonization refers to the historical and political resistance to colonization and the subsequent liberation of colonies after World War II.[2] However, this definition does not exhaust what decolonization entails. Theorists of both decoloniality[3] and postcolonialism[4] claim to be busy with epistemological decolonization. This is thus decolonization of the mind or a secondary, ideological resistance against colonization.

Mignolo places the difference between decoloniality and postcolonialism as follows: "The de-colonial shift . . . is a project of de-linking while post-colonial criticism and theory is a project of scholarly transformation within the academy."[5] Thus, Mignolo contends that decoloniality goes beyond postcolonialism's scholarly transformation. It is a "delinking that leads to de-colonial epistemic shift and brings to the foreground other epistemologies, other principles of knowledge and understanding and,

---

1. See Jiménez, "Towards a Postcolonial Homiletic"; Travis, *Decolonizing Preaching*; Pui-lan, "Postcolonial Preaching in Intercultural Contexts."
2. Said, *Culture and Imperialism*; Mignolo, "Delinking," 503.
3. Mignolo, "Delinking," 452.
4. Said, *Culture and Imperialism*, 209.
5. Mignolo, "Delinking," 452.

consequently, other economy [sic], other politics, other ethics."⁶ However, Lartey⁷ (referring to Edward Said) proposes that postcolonialism as a form of scholarly criticism is not a-practical, and, thus not merely an academic endeavor. In a similar vein to Mignolo's decoloniality, Lartey's postcolonialism is "life-enhancing and constitutively opposed to every form of tyranny, domination, and abuse, its social goals are non-coercive knowledge produced in the interests of human freedom."⁸ At the same time, Bhabha is adamant that the *post* in postcoloniality "only embod[ies] its restless and revisionary energy if [it] transform[s] the present into an expanded and ex-centric site of experience and empowerment."⁹

Although there is thus ambiguity between "decolonization," "decoloniality," "postcoloniality," and "postcolonialism," my choice for the term *postcolonial* is a choice for academic, systemic, and conscious decolonization. In other terms, I could have chosen one of the other terms, but chose to focus on the *post* of postcolonial as a transcending of, and a moving beyond, the colonial.

MY LOCATION OF CULTURE

At the same time, I believe it is important to state my own subjective and historical location of culture or positionality for this endeavor of engaging postcolonial thought. After all, as a white male in South Africa, my positionality could be perceived as problematic in this endeavor. Moreover, as Vuyani Vellem proposes, an excellent place to start is to "'disclose your location and assumptions upfront [sic],' in order to contribute with humility and responsibility."¹⁰

When South Africa became a democracy, I was three-and-a-half years old. Until the age of ten, I lived on a farm in a town named Vrede (Afrikaans for *peace*) in the Free State province. I have sometimes endeavored to determine how the land in Vrede came to be under my family's ownership. However, I have been met with both uncertainty and hostility for engaging in such a line of interrogation. Because of financial difficulties on the farm, family tensions, and the prospects of making a better life elsewhere, my

6. Mignolo, "Delinking," 452–53.
7. Lartey, *Postcolonializing God*, ix–x.
8. Lartey, *Postcolonializing God*, ix–x.
9. Bhabha, *Location of Culture*, 4.
10. Vellem, "Un-Thinking the West," 1.

Introduction

parents moved to Standerton at the beginning of 2001. In all aspects, my childhood was normal for a young white boy of those years; my friends were white, I called older white people *Oom* (uncle) and *Tannie* (aunt), and I understood black people to be of a different class, not part of *my* community.

However, a fundamental change in my lived experience occurred in 2009, my first year as a theology student at the University of the Free State (UFS). With the implementation of racial integration in the UFS residences, I became the only white resident in the Villa Bravado residence. To be clear, I was not the only white student placed in Villa Bravado; I was the only one who showed up and lived there.

In retrospect, my journey towards the moment I moved into Villa Bravado and the subsequent three years of calling it my home seems almost as if out of a novel. When I received the letter that I had been placed in Villa Bravado at the end of 2008, I was bombarded with warnings from elders and peers: "It is a black residence; you cannot live there." My parents, time and again, warned me, begged me, and proposed alternatives. My answer consisted of certainty that I would live there: after all, I had been given accommodation on campus, it was close to my classes, and my Christian understanding was that all people are equal before God. Villa Bravado subverted all the expectations of my parents. I was treated with respect and dignity by all students in Villa Bravado. I was included in all the residence activities, and after my culture shock subsided, I stopped thinking about racial differences. In my second year, I served on the Residence Committee, six months as vice-prime and six as prime.

Honestly, my presence in Villa Bravado made very little difference to the integration process. At the end of my first year, I was able to recruit three other white students to live as senior students in Villa Bravado, and we were able to recruit twenty white first-years to become residents in Villa Bravado. For perspective, Villa Bravado can accommodate 160 students. Although the white first-year students showed up, they all left by the second semester. This phenomenon was an unfortunate experience for the whole of Villa Bravado. During those times, it was understood as a failure of the residence when integration did not work. I cannot recall exactly what happened in my third year because I distanced myself from the residence management. However, integration worked very well. And by my fourth year, when I no longer lived in Villa Bravado, the residence received an award for the best strides in integration.

Irrelevant of the exact implications my stay in Villa Bravado had on the residence, it significantly impacted who I became.[11] For the first time, I made friends with people whose lived experiences were entirely different from mine. I heard stories of suffering and survival which I did not think possible. I became invested in the lives of my fellow housemates, irrelevant of cultural, linguistic, and racial differences. I relinquished so many prejudices about those I once thought were subaltern to myself, whom I had been told were primitive. I realized that all people were merely trying to make their way in this world.

Looking back, my experience in Villa Bravado paved the way for me to forge an identity outside my race's confines, loyalties, and expectations. In 2014, I chose to do a mini dissertation for my masters in divinity on the theology and sermons of Allan Boesak.[12] From Boesak, I learned a deep appreciation for Black Theology of Liberation, specifically the contextual and biblical hermeneutics from the starting point of the marginalized, weak, and excluded. Along with the influence the Confession of Belhar had on me, in 2016, I decided to accept a call to the Uniting Reformed Church (URCSA) Immanuel Standerton, once again working against my (so-called) white privilege by associating with those who would be perceived as "others" by some white people. I served as minister of word and sacrament at the Immanuel URCSA congregation in Standerton for two years.

However, my association with the experience of poverty was always in a proxy fashion. Some of Standerton's URCSA congregation members lived in extreme poverty, while I lived with my wife in relative comfort. I saw poverty and experienced its effects on the bodies of others, but I was, to a great extent, a mere observer. That is, until the end of 2018. At that time, I lost everything. My marriage ended, I resigned from my position

---

11. On contemplating my journey within Villa Bravado residence and the academic environment, I wonder about the possibility of a white (male) South African transcending the mindset, experiences, and expectations of the white community without an experience similar to the immersion I experienced in Villa Bravado. I think there are two sides to the influence this immersion had on me. Firstly, who I became was only possible because of this alternative space. Secondly, I was not the only one with the opportunity to be immersed in this space. Others were also given the opportunity but never embraced it. The first represents, on the one hand, the need for such spaces. Without alternative spaces, spaces of negotiation, we cannot transcend our upbringing. The second represents the (un)willingness to participate in these spaces. The existence of these spaces does not automatically bring forth the desire to participate therein. Stated differently, there is a catch-22 to the issue of whiteness in South Africa.

12. Wessels, "Preaching in South Africa Today."

Introduction

at the church (subsequently losing my legitimation status). Were it not for the unconditional friendship of colleagues in academia, I would have opted out of theology. For the first time, I experienced failure, fear, trauma, and poverty. I lived with my family for a few months, sleeping on a bed in the living room. I experienced the suffering of unemployment, the depression of having no purpose, and envy for those whose lives seemed to be going well. At the same time, however, I could achieve more than I expected of myself. I was welcomed by friends and strangers, not as a failure, but with love, and I became a more empathetic human being.

My self-understanding changed rapidly. With the experience of failing so miserably in life, I could not associate my theological training with my lived experience. Even though I knew about grace and often spoke about grace in sermons (claiming that God's grace was for everyone, even the drunkard, the criminal, and the gambler), I never genuinely expected that I would require God's grace. In my mind, grace was intended for others, not for me. And I thought I could live my life so that my righteousness would surpass the need for grace. However, it was only in my lived experience of being utterly forsaken by God through my shortcomings that I realized how much I needed and will always need God's grace.

Nevertheless, these experiences, in their opposites, brought forth questions about my own whiteness and maleness. As much as I could associate with others and experience the alterity of real suffering, was my white maleness a mask of privilege, a valid reason to disregard myself as legitimate in the conversation around decolonization, and to be disregarded by others? Steve Biko's critique against "white liberals" rings true in my ears, and I would certainly want to adhere to his call for white people to "serve as a lubricating material so that we [can] change the gears in trying to find a better direction for South Africa."[13]

Stated differently, I have endeavored to ask what John De Gruchy asked at *The 8th Steve De Gruchy Memorial Lecture* on April 30, 2019, "Is It Possible for a White South African Male to Enter the Kingdom of Heaven?":

> White South Africans cannot change in isolation from black South Africans. You cannot become a champion of justice if you are not enabled to see injustice through the eyes of those who experience it; you cannot become a worker for liberation if you do not experience something of the pain of oppression. You cannot really hear the gospel in a life-changing way if you only hear it from white

---

13. Biko, *Write What I Like*, 20–27.

voices. You cannot overcome fear of the other if you never meet and come to know the other. . . . There are lots of them, young, white male South Africans willing to engage in shaping a better future, and willing to share what they have received for the benefit of us all.[14]

I hope that my contemplation of postcolonial thought for preaching will simultaneously be an openness to learning from scholars different from me and my attempt to shape homiletics for preaching, which seeks out a better future for South Africa.

DOMINANT HOMILETIC THOUGHT IN SOUTH AFRICA

This brings me to the current state of homiletics in South Africa. For my master's thesis in 2016, I researched the trends in South African homiletics from 1974 to 2015.[15] The research is published in a chapter cowritten with Martin Laubscher as *A Prophetic Word on Studies in Prophetic Preaching? Re-visioning Prophetic Preaching's (Post)Apartheid Condition*. Herein we claim that prophetic preaching has become dominant in South African homiletic thought since the early 2010s.[16] We traced the coinage of prophetic preaching in South African homiletics back to Hennie Pieterse's 1995 book, *Desmond Tutu's Message: A Qualitative Analysis*. The definition we attributed to prophetic preaching was: "prophetic preaching is conceived in South Africa as preaching which is keenly aware and takes serious[ly] the ethical-political-societal dimensions of preaching."[17]

From this understanding of prophetic preaching, the agenda for academic homiletics in democratic South Africa became poverty relief through development.

> [L]iberation theology and prophetic preaching should guide the churches' contribution to the struggle for LIBERATION FROM POVERTY through reconstruction and development.[18]

---

14. De Gruchy, "Is It Possible?," 8–9.
15. Wessels, "Prophetic Preaching's (Post)Apartheid Condition."
16. Laubscher and Wessels, "Prophetic Word on Studies?," 182.
17. Laubscher and Wessels, "Prophetic Word on Studies?," 178.
18. Pieterse, "Prophetic Preaching in Context," 97.

INTRODUCTION

Pieterse builds upon this agenda by proposing that the goal of preaching is "to inspire the faithful with hope, and the courage to tackle the situation of poverty, and work for a better future."[19] Furthermore, there is a need for a type of "missionary diaconate," where the "church *for* the poor" is to aid the "church *of* the poor" in this endeavor of poverty relief.[20] Although, in more recent years, Pieterse entertains the possibility that all preaching is prophetic "in general terms," he returns to the proposal he made in 1995—that prophetic preaching is "from the angle of the poor . . . in terms of their need for justice and righteousness" with the "hermeneutical orientation" of responding to "the prevailing situation of poverty."[21]

Similarly, Cas Vos locates the hermeneutical starting point of preaching as the position of the poor, whereby "all ideologies that weaken and jeopardize the position of the poor" should be called out.[22] Furthermore, preaching's goal should aid in such a manner that "listeners are able to respond obediently and transform their situation [of poverty] positively and through action."[23]

So too, proposes Allan Boesak that preaching should be an "embrace of the struggles of the poor and the powerless."[24] However, Boesak's proposal does not include the idea that the goal of preaching becomes poverty relief, either by the rich for the poor as charity nor as self-development of the poor. He instead opts to speak against the capitalist system, claiming that it is a kingdom in opposition to the kingdom of God. Therefore, he claims, "the world as it is is *wrong*."[25] Instead, he proposes that Christians should participate "in acts of liberation and justice in the dreaded places of fear and trepidation where the powers believe they hold sway."[26]

Other scholars in South African homiletics choose to take a position that is harder to pinpoint, in my opinion, because their chosen position tries to be *neutral*. However, as far as I am concerned, they propose the

---

19. Pieterse, "Communicative Rationality and Hermeneutical Insights," 557.

20. Pieterse, "Communicative Rationality and Hermeneutical Insights"; Costas, "Evangelism and the Gospel," 33.

21. Pieterse, "Prophetic Preaching in the Contemporary Context," 5.

22. Vos, "Drivers for the Writing," 302.

23. Vos, "Drivers for the Writing," 302.

24. Boesak, "'Hope Unprepared to Accept Things,'" 1060.

25. Boesak, *Kairos, Crisis, and Global Apartheid*, 122.

26. Boesak, *Kairos, Crisis, and Global Apartheid*, 122.

same paradigm as playing by the rules of capitalist development and poverty relief.

Ian Nell proposes that preaching, in a theodrama paradigm, should aid the church "to live (i.e. act out) the story of salvation for the world."[27] He places two markers for this goal; that the church is "the stage where God's drama is played out" and that Christians must, as a responsibility, participate in this drama towards the renewal of the world.[28] There is no explicit or implicit questioning of systemic injustice or the legacy of apartheid. Instead, there is merely a comment that the theodrama "applies equally to the challenges facing the churches within the current South African context."[29] Which challenges? For which church(es)?

In 2017, Nell contemplated the theodrama paradigm once more. This time his starting position was the proposal of the British theologian David Ford that "the dramatic and therefore performative aspects of Christian theology" should be privileged for the future of Christian theology.[30] Firstly, I wonder how relevant Ford's proposal is to the South African context. Once more, Nell proposes the theodrama as an answer to Ford's call; theodrama as God's invitation to the Christian community to "partake in the drama of life."[31] Yet, nowhere does he clarify the hermeneutical pointers of interpretation for what he means by the drama of life. Whose theodrama? He could claim it is God's drama, but who is responsible for interpreting what is part of God's drama and what is not? Is this God of drama neutral? Or does this God choose sides? Is it merely *our* (whoever our group or enclave is) drama of life? What about the drama or lived experiences of the *other*?

Moreover, even if he proposes that God is the primary actor, who decides what we have heard from God as the primary plot of the drama? What are the implications of the silence on matters of contextualization? And if there is silence on contextual matters, what does salvation mean within the theodrama?

Similarly, de Wet and Kruger contemplate prophetic preaching in general, neutral terms, stating, "Preaching that ministers the Word of the eternal God to a society in need of change and destined for change can be

---

27. Nell, "In Search of Meaning," 571.
28. Nell, "In Search of Meaning," 571.
29. Nell, "In Search of Meaning," 572.
30. Nell, "Preaching and Performance," 309–10.
31. Nell, "Preaching and Performance," 318.

Introduction

defined as prophetic preaching."[32] What exactly is meant by change? Moreover, they believe prophetic preaching should equip "Christians to . . . [refocus] the world on its destiny in a restored relationship with God."[33] Once more, is it possible to make such bold claims in a neutral manner, especially as white South African males who both trained and wrote theologically during the apartheid years? Moreover, is it possible to make such claims as if in a neutral manner from the positionality of the North-West University's Potchefstroom campus? Or at least, how can it take a neutral stance without even naming your positionality today and historically?

In another article, the late Fritz de Wet proposes that prophetic preaching should be an increasing awareness of "God's vision for this world" from the hermeneutical orientation of a "heart that is in the process of being purified by God's grace."[34] From this awareness and orientation of the heart, de Wet believes reality can be named for what it is, and a prophetic vision for the future can be preached. I believe this proposal of de Wet represents the most esoteric proposal for prophetic preaching. How is this awareness determined or underpinned? How is it determined whether or not a process of purification is taking place? Is not all preaching then prophetic, irrelevant of all matters, when God is actively purifying the hearts of all the faithful? What about explicit and implicit agendas on the pulpit, even of people with seemingly pure hearts? And should we then even contemplate preaching? From another perspective, what is the pedagogy for teaching preaching in such a manner?

My discomfort with a neutral position regarding academic homiletics is twofold. First, I do not think such a thing as a neutral position exists, and to claim such a position is a myth. Secondly, a neutral position, in my opinion, merely underscores the status quo. Without explicit contextual analysis, it implies that the prevailing systems must be acceptable at best and God-ordained at worst. Either way, neither preaching will shy away from the political and the public. It will be private and spiritualized.

During the time in which prophetic preaching became an essential concept in homiletics, Cilliers wrote *The Living Voice of the Gospel*. Herein, Cilliers develops a theory for homiletics which he summarizes as follows:

---

32. De Wet and Kruger, "Blessed Are Those That Hunger," 1.
33. De Wet and Kruger, "Blessed Are Those That Hunger," 7.
34. De Wet, "Naming and Nurturing Reality," 8.

> Preaching takes place when God's voice is heard through the voice of the text, in the voice of the time (congregation context), through the (unique) voice of the preacher. When these four voices become one voice, then the sermon is indeed *viva vox evangelii*.[35]

Cilliers builds his homiletic theory around these four aspects of preaching: theology, hermeneutics, contextualization, and the person(ality) of the preacher.[36] This study of Cilliers, per earlier work, focuses on the ethics of preaching, how preaching can either be the living voice of the gospel, giving life and speaking the good news, or moralism, binding life and instilling fear. In a 2018 interview, Cilliers made the following remark:

> I started out with a fascination for the worlds and dynamics of written texts, in particular also for the destructive elements thereof. So, I started to discover how dangerous for instance, preaching can be—if it creates and defends destructive agendas such as apartheid. Moralism could also be linked to texts that bind and judge, that instill fear and create enclaves; that enslave within the rigid laws of some forms of religion.[37]

What Cilliers does when it comes to prophetic preaching, rather than following in Pieterse's footsteps, is to interpret Black Theology of Liberation for himself. He understands that Black Theology of Liberation's image of God stands next to the weak in society and showcases God's foolishness and weakness, and claims that the preacher should follow in this foolishness of God.[38] The implication is that the political status quo, even democracy, cannot merely be interpreted as God's will, nor can anyone state that preaching is supposed to cling to the agendas of poverty relief and development. After all, God's association with the poor, marginalized, and subaltern represents a foolish subversion to the status quo. In my opinion, Cilliers, albeit implicitly, represents a postcolonial direction within South African homiletics.

With his focus on the ethics of preaching, Cilliers goes on to interpret a sermon of Allan Boesak in a completely different way to the expected conclusion that it is a prophetic sermon. He starts by stating that the sermon "could justifiably be called *prophetic preaching that strives to address a concrete situation*" but concludes that the situation of apartheid overpowers

---

35. Cilliers, *Living Voice of the Gospel*, 32.
36. See Cilliers, *Uitwissing van God op die kansel*.
37. Cilliers and Laubscher, "Interview with Prof. Johan Cilliers," 7.
38. Cilliers, "Clown before the Powers"; Cilliers, "Clowning on the Pulpit?"; Cilliers, "Preaching as Reframing of Perspective," 90.

Introduction

the gospel in the sermon and turns the sermon into a moralistic exercise.[39] Cilliers makes the following claim:

> This then becomes [Boesak's] intention with his sermon: to bring God back into the picture, and the way to achieve this is by calling on the Christians in South Africa to act in such a manner that God can again be (experienced as) present in the South African situation.[40]

Once more, in this demonstration of Cilliers, so-called prophetic preaching can be just another form of moralization. Put another way, if God is taken out of the picture of a sermon, even if it is political and speaks against societal injustices, only the human endeavor of bettering the world remains. After all, the exact opposite is also true; if ethics and human responsibility are taken out of the picture, the status quo becomes equated with God's will.

His most striking critique against prophetic preaching (and some other types of moralizing sermons), however, are these words:

> God in fact . . . is changed by the sermon from present and active to absent and inactive. This *image of the absent and inactive God* is underlined by the stereotypical structure of religious activism (see Cilliers 1996:98) . . ., which would be described in a nutshell as follows: 1. God did (in the past) 2. God wants to (in the future) 3. We must (in the present).[41]

Again, for Cilliers, religious activism exterminates God from the pulpit,[42] irrelevant to the perspective from where the sermon is preached, be it to sustain the status quo or to dismantle the status quo.

Fortunately, Cilliers does not only critique prophetic preaching. He also proposes a definition of prophetic preaching, which takes God seriously as the primary actor in life. Cilliers states that prophetic preaching is the evoking of the experience of anticipation of new creation breaking forth within the old creation through what God does and will do.[43][44]

39. Cilliers, "Prophetic Preaching in South Africa," 9.
40. Cilliers, "Prophetic Preaching in South Africa," 9.
41. Cilliers, "Disabling God?," 5. Original italics.
42. Here I am explicitly referring to Cilliers, *Uitwissing van God op die kansel*; Cilliers, *God for Us?* Cilliers' discomfort with moralism (religious activism) is palpable throughout his writings.
43. Cilliers, "Where Have All the Prophets Gone?," 378–9.
44. As I understand Cilliers' homiletics, he is deeply concerned that God should be

Postcolonial Homiletics?

In the conclusion of this book, I will converse more thoroughly with the current academic thoughts in South African homiletics. For now, however, I propose that prophetic preaching as the dominant system of thought for South African homiletics is a form of academic colonization of Black Theology of Liberation (BTL).

There should be no question about the intention of homiletic scholars in South Africa regarding prophetic preaching. I am convinced their intentions are indeed pure. However, as the academic environment endeavors to be a space of scholarly negotiation and is always open to critique, I am convinced that the proposal of prophetic preaching is problematic, even colonial.

It is undoubtedly true that homiletic contemplation on prophetic preaching tries to be transformative within the context of democratic South Africa. However, beneath the good intentions of the homiletic academia, white scholars have been attempting to position themselves in such a manner as to maintain advantage "in a situation in which black people have legally and legitimately achieved political power."[45] Again, without admitting that BTL was ignored during the apartheid years and (even) explicitly condemned,[46] the homiletic fraternity embraces BTL as *the paradigm* for preaching in democratic South Africa.[47] Moreover, with an agenda for poverty relief and development, which does not take the radical claims of BTL seriously, we seem to be misrepresenting BTL.[48]

In an attempt to be generous about studies of prophetic preaching, de Oliveira Andreotti et al. help to make sense.[49] They propose that epistemological transformation could take on the character of soft-reform where the emphasis is on "the rights and responsibilities of individuals to determine their own success or failure, as measured by the values of the existing (and

---

the primary actor within the sermon. However, with regards to how this primary action interacts with ethics and the church's interaction within South African social realities, much is left unanswered. What is the relationship between preaching and human agency, especially that of the faith community? What about the liturgy after the liturgy? What is the relationship between moralism and ethics? Furthermore, what would be the relationship between the God-event of Cilliers' homiletics and human agency in society; if any?

45. Steyn and Foster, "Repertoires for Talking White," 26.
46. See Smith, *Kansel en Politiek*.
47. See Laubscher and Wessels, "Prophetic Word on Studies?"
48. With the implication that the *people* are not embraced by South African homiletics.
49. De Oliveira Andreotti et al., "Mapping Interpretations of Decolonization."

INTRODUCTION

taken for granted) system."⁵⁰ In this sense, the rules of the dominant system are not questioned, and there is a mere proposal that success depends on the individual's ability to pull themselves up from the bootstraps.

As de Oliveira Andreotti et al. show, the difference between what has happened in South African homiletics (soft-reform) and what has been called for by Black theologians (radical-reform) "is a recognition of epistemological dominance."⁵¹ The first does not recognize, while the latter recognizes epistemological dominance. Nowhere does post-apartheid South African homiletics identify or contemplate epistemological dominance. Radical-reform, in opposition, calls for "a more drastic interruption of business-as-usual."⁵²

POSTCOLONIAL PREACHING?

Returning to the center of this book, I endeavor to engage with postcolonial theory from a practical theological position focusing on homiletics. My central research question is: What would a theory of homiletics which takes postcolonial theory seriously possess? Or, in short: Postcolonial Homiletics?

To answer this question, I have divided this book into five chapters.

In the first chapter, I endeavor to articulate concretely what I mean by *postcolonial*. It is, therefore, a chapter dedicated to defining concepts. I begin with Black Theology of Liberation (BTL), which possesses postcolonial ideas. At the same time, I have delimited where postcolonial theory deviates from BTL.

In the second chapter, I discuss homiletic theory and postcolonial theory. The first movement is the contemplation of some homiletic theories. After that, as the second movement, I place a preliminary postcolonial theory for homiletics on the table. Lastly, I attempt a postcolonial sermon.

In the third chapter, I look at the potential of a postcolonial liturgy. This is also a conversation between current streams and thoughts about liturgy and postcolonial thought, as I delimited in chapter 2. From here, I place route markers for a postcolonial liturgy. Lastly, I attempt a postcolonial liturgy.

---

50. De Oliveira Andreotti et al., "Mapping Interpretations of Decolonization," 26.
51. De Oliveira Andreotti et al., "Mapping Interpretations of Decolonization," 26.
52. De Oliveira Andreotti et al., "Mapping Interpretations of Decolonization," 26.

In chapter 4, I contemplate postcolonial theory and hermeneutics concerning the interpretation of the Bible for postcolonial preaching. Taking Acts 10, I consider three focal images of postcolonial thought to shift the center of hermeneutics and open new possibilities for interpreting the text.

In the fifth and final chapter, I return to the landscape of South African homiletics. Here I endeavor a postcolonial reflection on the two major streams in South African homiletics: prophetic preaching and aesthetics.

CHAPTER 1

Genealogical Comparison between Black Theology of Liberation (BTL) and Postcolonial Thought

AT THE ANNUAL CONFERENCE of the Society of Practical Theology in South Africa in 2017, with the theme of *Decolonizing Practical Theology in South Africa*, I was struck by the experience of repeatedly hearing Black Theology of Liberation (BTL) equated with decolonization. Bowers Du Toit stood out as a prominent example herein. She claimed that her "paper highlights the manner in which BC [Black Consciousness] and Black Theology could provide the opportunity for decolonized praxis that recognizes the importance of indigenous identity and self-reliance, centers the local community and forms part of larger movements for justice and liberation."[1]

Stated differently, BTL was identified as the epistemological carrier of decolonization. However, at the same time, postcolonial thinkers such as Homi Bhabha, Gayatri Spivak, Edward Said, Aníbal Quijano, Walter Mignolo, Ngũgĩ wa Thiong'o, and Frantz Fanon did not feature in the conference.

The first question which came to my mind was: Is there a difference between BTL and postcolonial thought? The second: What would it mean to consider postcolonial scholars who have been excluded in the practical theological conversation seriously? I will try to answer these questions through a genealogical overview of BTL on the one hand and postcolonial theory on the other.

1. Bowers du Toit, "Decolonising Development?," 33.

BLACK THEOLOGY OF LIBERATION—GENEALOGICAL OVERVIEW

To give a historical overview of Black Theology of Liberation (BTL), I have decided to focus on BTL in South Africa, taking cognizance that South African BTL's relation to the global movements of Liberation Theology is similar and different. However, the scope of global Liberation Theology is merely too much for this project. I will give this overview by tracing thoughts in the Journal of Black Theology in South Africa from 1987 to 1989, as well as some Black Theological thought since the dawn of a democratic South Africa.

Black Theology of Liberation during Apartheid

Maimela proposes that BTL during apartheid emphasized four themes: "The World Is in Conflict between the Oppressor and the Oppressed," "Theology Must Take a Preferential Option for the Oppressed," "Salvation as Historical Social Fact," and "The World Is History-in-the-Making."[2] From a different perspective, but also essential to notice, Motlhabi names four sources for BTL: "the Bible, the black experience, the black church, and the influence of African culture."[3]

In my attempt to present a manageable tracing of BTL during apartheid building upon Maimela and Motlhabi (notwithstanding the apparent shortcomings any manageable tracing will have), I propose three markers for BTL during apartheid. One, the black experience as the hermeneutic point of departure. Two, a commitment to BTL as theology which takes the black experience seriously as the hermeneutic point of departure. And three, real-world socioeconomic liberation for the black community.

The Black Experience as the Hermeneutic Point of Departure

> Black people have been dispossessed of their land which is the basic means of all production and subsistence as well as a source of power. —Takatso Mofokeng[4]

---

2. Maimela, "Current Themes and Emphases," 101–12.
3. Motlhabi, "Historical Origins of Black Theology," 41.
4. Mofokeng, "Following the Trail," 24.

> Black theology's starting point, therefore, is an economically, politically, culturally and morally dispossessed people. It carries with it the morality and social assumptions of a people who have suffered the hypocrisy of a supposedly superior civilization. —Itumeleng Mosala[5]

Naming black experience in its contextual reality is firstly a naming of the oppression of black existence. Even more, this naming of reality thoroughly is understood in BTL as a crucial task to "hear the 'new word of God' in the present."[6] Thus, the position of the black experience as the hermeneutic point of departure is, from the outset, a theological task.

BTL clearly and concisely names oppression as a systemic "domination of black people" by the white oppressor and the apartheid government-sanctioned violence through "rubber bullets and buckshot . . . handgrenades and petrol bombs."[7] Ngcokovane rightly shows that this situation is a situation of people being robbed of freedom by massive structures of society.[8] Once more, there is no space for generalities; to consider the black experience seriously is to concisely and particularly interpret and name the context. Mofokeng shows how the land has "forcibly and illegally [been] stolen" from black people.[9] Furthermore, this dispossession is an economic activity that determines the oppression, lack of means of production, and powerlessness of black people, as well as the economic flourishing of whites.[10]

From the position of the black experience, there is a clear vision that capitalism creates chaos, destroying products that could have been used by the same people producing these products. However, in the interest of ascertaining profits, this does not happen.[11]

Motlhabi opines that the "so-called black problem" consists of three main questions for the white government; how to dispossess black people of their land without regression, how to exploit black labor without reasonable compensation, and how to tax black people without political

---

5. Mosala, "Black Theology," 32–34.
6. Ramose, "Two Hands of God," 19.
7. Mofokeng, "Black Christology," 1.
8. Ngcokovane, "Ethical Problems," 27.
9. Mofokeng, "Black Christology," 10.
10. Mofokeng, "Following the Trail," 24.
11. Mosala, "Christianity and Socialism," 33.

representation.[12] "All this amounted to wishing that black people were mere zombies who provided all the needs of white people but remained dispensable in all other respects."[13] All forms of social services and services administrated by the government followed this trend of being exceptionally backward and inadequate for black people.[14] At the same time, black as a term in the South African context is also an overarching term for all indigenous South African people. Thus the black experience is an experience of a colonized people.[15]

Even within religion, the rules are different from a position of blackness. There is no "covenant with their Creator and enjoy[ment] of God's blessing[s]"; there is only a life of "concrete misery and constant reminder that they are . . . non-persons."[16] From birth, black people are made to understand that they are not made in God's image but God's "negative image . . . their life is a negative anthropology itself."[17] It became the church's role in South African society to legitimize "the sociopolitical and economic interests of whites at the expense of the oppressed Black majority."[18] Even the missionaries who sometimes stood up for indigenous South Africans would not hesitate to use violence when they thought it necessary to punish African kings who did not want to adhere to their agendas.[19] Moreover, the missionaries used the Bible in such a way as to oppress black people in South Africa, with the conviction that biblical texts sanctioned such oppression and made better slaves of black people.[20] Mofokeng admits that the Bible is a problem for BTL because it has been and can be used to justify oppression.[21]

Once more, Mofokeng showcases clearly that the theology of Afrikaners underscored and fostered colonialism by locating election and covenant amongst Afrikanerdom as if they were the new Israel who was not only

---

12. Motlhabi, "Black Resistance to Apartheid," 4–5.
13. Motlhabi, "Black Resistance to Apartheid," 5.
14. Sizwe, "Christian's Political Responsibility," 51.
15. Ramose, "Two Hands of God," 21.
16. Maimela, "What Do the Churches Want?," 44.
17. Mofokeng, "Cross in the Search," 45.
18. Maimela, "Theological Dilemmas and Options," 18.
19. Mofokeng, "Black Christians, the Bible," 35.
20. Mofokeng, "Black Christians, the Bible," 46.
21. Mofokeng, "Black Christians, the Bible," 46.

led by God but also led towards the new promised land—South Africa.[22] This implied that Afrikaners' Christian mission endeavors amongst black people always comprised superiority and unequal relations.[23] Conversely, oppression, discrimination, and exclusion from white Christianity brought forth the understanding that black people and black people "alone are indeed born in sin and are not worthy of the love and grace of God."[24] Again, Afrikaner theology has created a "system of self-justification, self-salvation and self-preservation on the basis of which White people are given life in all its fullness while Blacks are condemned to intolerable socio-political existence."[25]

The effect of Afrikaner and white theology on blackness has been severely traumatic. As Khabela points out, black communities have not only been disrupted, but the black religious experience is fraught with stress, strain, negative influence, fear, and ambivalence, "resulting in a fragmented self . . . in a perpetual conflict of insecurity in society."[26] Furthermore, black Christians in mainline churches ("white churches") have traumatic doublethink, where they are neither black nor white enough.[27] This results in a situation where identity is lost without an awareness of the loss of identity.

Yet, and this, I believe, is paramount, the black experience in a white world is not only that of being oppressed. Black people, even within oppression, find power through movements, organization, and struggle. Stated differently, the black experience is also an experience of concretely working towards a change in the context and situation. One such understanding of living as a struggle is intertwined with the secular philosophy of Black Consciousness.[28] BTL, too, intertwined this understanding under the influences of Black Consciousness.[29] Furthermore, the knowledge of the identity of black people changed; black people were now seen as workers. Thus the struggle moved beyond a struggle against racism towards a struggle for human, social, political, and economic rights.[30]

22. Mofokeng, "Cross in the Search," 38.
23. Mofokeng, "Cross in the Search," 38.
24. Mofokeng, "Cross in the Search," 45.
25. Maimela, "Faith That Does Justice," 7.
26. Khabela, "Socio-Cultural Dynamics," 23.
27. Khabela, "Socio-Cultural Dynamics," 34.
28. Motlhabi, "Black Resistance to Apartheid," 9.
29. Mosala, "Implications of the Text"; Muzorewa, "African Liberation Theology," 57.
30. Mofokeng, "Following the Trail," 24.

Once more, BTL's insistence that the contextuality of the situation of the black experience is paramount is not a knee-jerk reaction or being overwhelmed by the situation; it is a theological imperative. As Mofokeng states, "Conversely by being true Christians of our time and our locality, we are being true to the legacy of the New Testament communities. And conversely, by ignoring our time, our locality and its challenges we are being unworthy heirs of this noble Christian tradition."[31]

This brings me to a second point, the black experience as the hermeneutic point of departure brings forth a theological interpretation of God and the church as partakers in the black experience.

> God has not just become man. God has become oppressed man.
> —Takatso Mofokeng[32]

From the black hermeneutic point of departure, there exists a vociferous understanding that God reveals Godself as "the poor Jew from Galilee" which translates in the South African apartheid context as "black in South Africa."[33] Thus, God's revelation is understood not merely as God partaking in the human condition, but God participating in a specific type of human experience, one of the poverty, oppression, and suffering of the "bodies of black people of this country."[34] Moreover, as Mofokeng proposes, to understand what is "happening to God and to Jesus in South Africa today," we should look at how black people are mistreated, even crucified.[35] Stated otherwise, God becomes so intertwined in the black experience that God's very existence in the present becomes and is that of contemporary black suffering under apartheid.

Furthermore, in what I believe is an exceptional, contextual naming of whom the church constitutes, black hermeneutics shows that the church is indeed a black church. Most members of mainline and independent churches in South Africa (except for the Dutch Reformed Church) are black.[36] However, here comes the crux of the matter, theologically and structurally: the power of the mainline churches is concretely in the hands

---

31. Mofokeng, "Black Christology," 3.
32. Mofokeng, "Black Christology," 15.
33. Mofokeng, "Black Christology," 15.
34. Mofokeng, "Black Christology," 15.
35. Mofokeng, "Cross in the Search," 46.
36. Maimela, "Theological Dilemmas and Options," 16.

of white people.[37] This implies that "the Black church is thus a colonized and dominated church theologically and culturally because it has inherited all the theological slogans and expressions from our white mentors."[38] What BTL endeavors for and what Maimela calls for is the construction of a new theology which takes note of the experiential nature of the church as oppressed and impoverished.

From a different perspective, the understanding of BTL is that hermeneutical similarities exist between the black church and the communities spoke of in biblical revelation to such an extent that the black church should be privileged in interpreting the Bible.[39] Even more, this contextualization of the black church is a reclaiming of "the basic tenets of Christianity."[40] The positioning of God amongst the black community and claiming the church to be black is, in essence, a matter of an orthodox interpretation of Christianity and the Bible.

Finally, the black experience as the hermeneutic point of departure calls forth a rethinking of the relationship between African culture and Christianity.

> Christianity must have a truly African character if it is to remain in Africa, and be the religion of Africa. —SIGQIBO DWANE[41]

From the onset of theological engagement from the black experience, it is clear that a rethinking must occur regarding the relationship between African culture and Christianity. The Christianity which, at this point, has been promoted in Africa is a Christianity that carries with it European culture. No, it insists that to be Christian is to be European. On the other hand, it is interesting that Mofokeng opines that African traditional religions can no longer claim to be hegemonic because Christianity has become such a driving force amongst Africans.[42] Put another way, although Christianity came to Africa through the Western missionary movements, it will be part of the future of African religion. He shows that, historically, two directions have been followed concerning the interaction between African traditional religions and Christianity. One is the course of African Independent

---

37. Maimela, "Theological Dilemmas and Options," 16.
38. Maimela, "Theological Dilemmas and Options," 16.
39. Mofokeng, "Black Christians, the Bible," 40.
40. Goba, "Toward a Quest," 33.
41. Dwane, "Gospel and Culture," 21.
42. Mofokeng, "Black Christians, the Bible," 36.

Churches, where a compromise has been struck between the Bible and African religion (without proper assimilation). Two, the direction of mainline churches where African religion has been obliterated, and European culture have been promoted as Christian.

From the black experience, however, theologians have been able to name the inconsistency of such an understanding of Christianity. A conversion to European Christianity has been merely the conversion to a theological language supporting the conqueror.[43] The proposal is instead that Christianity and African culture should go through a process of assimilation, much as it has gone through assimilating European culture.[44] Stated differently, to be genuinely African Christians, black Christians should understand "that there are riches in [their] own heritage, and [learn] to appreciate them."[45]

Goba states that a hermeneutical grounding of Christianity within African culture is the only way the church can be authentically Christian in Africa.[46] Dwane agrees, saying that a concrete and indigenized Christianity is the only way the church could be universal.[47] Its universality lies in taking root in the particular culture of blackness, not through the forced conversion to a supposedly global European culture.

Black Theology of Liberation

The second practice of BTL is the delimiting of what BTL is. I distinguish three tasks of delimiting BTL. These are the task of distinguishing BTL from white theology; the task of apologetics, claiming that BTL is a biblical imperative; and the task of constructing BTL as explicitly public and political.

Firstly, Black Theology of Liberation explicitly and concretely distinguishes itself from white theology.

> In fact, it is possible that this is what makes First World theologians restless when they hear the term "Liberation Theology." The term frightens many of them because they want to be in control even if it means not listening to the Holy Spirit. —Gwinyai Muzorewa[48]

43. Mofokeng, "Cross in the Search," 39.
44. Dwane, "Gospel and Culture," 20.
45. Dwane, "Gospel and Culture," 20.
46. Goba, "Toward a Quest," 35.
47. Dwane, "Gospel and Culture," 25.
48. Muzorewa, "African Liberation Theology," 55.

Comparison between (BTL) & Postcolonial Thought

BTL takes an explicit, concrete, and unapologetic stand against white theology by showcasing its theological understanding vis-à-vis white theology. As the first movement of this theological system breakage, BTL showcases white Christians and theologians' discomfort with understanding Jesus as poor.[49] After all, from a Black Theological perspective, it seems white theology insists that Jesus' position of culture has to coincide with a bourgeois background, the white social class, or Jesus must be colorless and neutral.[50] According to Mosala, there have been many attempts by what he calls "liberal scholarship" (white theologians) to prove that Jesus was not revolutionary.[51] Mosala is convinced that Jesus' politics are "a fundamental socialist ethic."[52] In the Lucan understanding of Jesus, doing good is "service for the victims of the structures of society and nature that shapes the vision of a liberated future."[53]

White theology is also plagued with its historic understanding of Christianity, where black people have been reduced to "inferior beings ... to nothingness."[54] This reduction of black people and the introduction of an economy of black slave labor have been fundamental in the partnership between colonialism and the Christian missionary endeavors in Africa.[55] Through all this, black Christians find themselves in a situation where faith and their experiences are incompatible. As Khabela states, a "schizophrenic religious feeling" exists amongst black Christians, where racial discrimination and cultural denigration are divinely ordained.[56] For white theology, religious pluralism and African culture are incompatible with Christianity. However, for BTL, there is "an open and dynamic view here that religious identity is something innovative and creative."[57] Yet and despite white theology, BTL has given black people the ability and power to disallow myths of inferiority and instead give hope within the situation of oppression and exploitation.[58]

---

49. Mofokeng, "Black Christology," 15.
50. Mofokeng, "Black Christology," 15.
51. Mosala, "Christianity and Socialism," 35–36.
52. Mosala, "Christianity and Socialism," 35.
53. Mosala, "Christianity and Socialism," 36.
54. Jordaan, "Emergence of Black Feminist Theology," 42–43.
55. Mofokeng, "Black Christians, the Bible," 34.
56. Khabela, "Socio-Cultural Dynamics," 26.
57. Goba, "Toward a Quest," 33.
58. Jordaan, "Emergence of Black Feminist Theology," 42–43.

Furthermore, as Maimela understands the existence, history, and method of white theology, there is a direct linkage between white theology and the "church allowing itself to be hijacked and taken over by the ruling class" since the Constantinian era.[59] The dislocation of justice and faith further underscores this, a dislocation Maimela believes lies in a breakage of the relationship between the church and the poor. This dislocation is an inevitable outcome in white theology as right believing and right doing are also dislocated. BTL, however, insists that there is no right believing without right doing.[60] BTL is, as Lamola defines it, "an epistemologically self-defined theological system, a phenomenon which is secondary to a consciousness of the reality of being black in a white racist world."[61] In other terms, a world created by white theology, with a normative stance for middle-class whiteness, creates the climate for BTL to protest against such a world. A contextual and situational interpretation of Christianity is paramount for BTL within a context of "suffering, estrangement, induced self-debasement and struggle of the Black people in South Africa."[62]

Once more, the situational location of doing theology is paramount for BTL and stands directly against white theology's insistence that the context should not overwhelm dogma. In this sense, BTL is ahead in understanding that doctrine (and the hermeneutics of systematic theology) is always dependent on a subjective position of perspective. Therefore, to do BTL is to "approach Scripture in search of what and how to think and articulate what is happening to them and their world."[63] From the experience of oppression and exploitation, black Christians could do nothing else but translate these experiences theologically.[64] It was necessary to create a theology that could liberate people from white theology within the context of the black lived experiences.[65] Thus, to do BTL is to search for theological insights, even within white theology, of value for the problems black people face in the context of apartheid.[66] In this personal, contextual experience of God, it can only be understood that God is not neutral. God is the God who

59. Maimela, "Theological Dilemmas and Options," 18.
60. Maimela, "Theological Dilemmas and Options," 24.
61. Lamola, "Thought of Steve Biko," 2.
62. Lamola, "Thought of Steve Biko," 3.
63. Mofokeng, "Black Christology," 2.
64. Mofokeng, "Black Christology," 8.
65. Muzorewa, "African Liberation Theology," 52.
66. Maimela, "Faith That Does Justice," 2.

takes sides; the side of the "oppressed, the downtrodden, the poor, and God acts violently against those who perform degrading acts of oppression."[67]

Moreover, since the reception of the Bible, black people have appropriated and interpreted the Bible within their situation. And to be precise, their hermeneutics has always been of selective use of the Bible, as far as the Bible was helpful in the liberation of the black position.[68] Interestingly, Mofokeng is under no illusion that the Bible is liberational, such that white theologians have misinterpreted the Bible.[69] Although he states that some texts have been misinterpreted, he clearly understands that others have been interpreted correctly and that those texts serve an oppressive agenda. Thus, the imperative is to identify liberational texts and use them "to the exclusion of others."[70]

The difference between BTL and white theology goes even further. Words and concepts have different meanings within the two theological constructs. As Maimela claims, "In short, even the word gospel will have different meanings for black and white churches."[71] When BTL speaks of liberation, it is both a response to human existential needs and a word about redemption.[72]

Furthermore, the concept of sin is not about the personal sin against God for BTL; sin is structural violence and the breakage of relationships amongst community members.[73] Maimela goes as far as to claim that "western definitions of what constitutes salvation should not be accepted."[74] For instance, Luther's *justification by faith alone* which speaks about assurance of forgiveness and everlasting life, should not be accepted without "heavy qualifications" because life after death is neither an African problem nor a problem facing the Black church in their context.[75] The placing of concerns over hell as central is thus detrimental to the ministry of the Black church in context. But even more, as Maimela correctly shows a bit later, Luther's concept of *justification by faith alone* meant that "now life was no longer

---

67. Jordaan, "Emergence of Black Feminist Theology," 44.
68. Mofokeng, "Black Christians, the Bible," 40.
69. Mofokeng, "Black Christians, the Bible," 37.
70. Mofokeng, "Black Christians, the Bible," 38.
71. Maimela, "What Do the Churches Want?," 43.
72. Ngcokovane, "Ethical Problems, Options and Strategies," 27.
73. Maimela, "Theological Dilemmas and Options," 16.
74. Maimela, "Theological Dilemmas and Options," 16.
75. Maimela, "Theological Dilemmas and Options," 23.

open to the few, the successful achievers who please God. Instead, life was now open to the weak, the poor, the powerless and the unsuccessful."[76] In Black Theological terms within the South African context during apartheid, *justification by faith* means "all human beings are unworthy, unacceptable, and sinners before God, and therefore that no race or group of people is any better than another"[77] and that all are accepted and allowed life only because of God's grace and mercy. Furthermore, Maimela showcases that justification and social justice are linked in Luther's thinking, and thus *justification by faith* is a call to work for justice in South Africa.[78]

Secondly, Black Theology of Liberation understands itself as a biblical imperative. To do BTL is to be obedient to the Bible.

> It is based on the historical fact that Jesus of Nazareth chose the side of the underdogs in society, lived a life of solidarity of the kingdom of God with the poor, the weak and the despised. — TAKATSO MOFOKENG[79]

> God has not just become man. God has become oppressed man. God has come as the black in the scarred and bleeding bodies of black people of this country. —TAKATSO MOFOKENG[80]

BTL understands that to do BTL is an obligation laid by God through the Bible upon the lived experience of struggle in South Africa. Stated otherwise, from a Christological basis, BTL must be done. Jesus as the poor man incarnate, the one on the side of the poor, the weak, and the despised, is God's "historical act of solidarity with man."[81] Thus, in apartheid South Africa the scriptural revelation in conversation with the lived experience and position of the culture of the black community is that "Jesus the poor Jew from Galilee is black in South Africa."[82] Mofokeng describes God as "the oppressed poor God . . . [and] the black in the scarred and bleeding bodies of black people." Even more, the suffering of Jesus enables the ability to "critically understand the suffering of the innocent in human history"

---

76. Maimela, "Faith That Does Justice," 5.
77. Maimela, "Faith That Does Justice," 7.
78. Maimela, "Faith That Does Justice," 11.
79. Mofokeng, "Black Christology," 4.
80. Mofokeng, "Black Christology," 15.
81. Mofokeng, "Black Christology," 4.
82. Mofokeng, "Black Christology," 15.

and evokes rage for this suffering, as well as the command to work against human suffering.[83]

As Moila states, Christology is militant. It is a call for revolutionary action of faith. It calls for an orthopraxis of "solidarity with the poor in fighting misery, oppression and injustice." It is a call for both the black community and all churches.[84] For BTL, the Christocentric understanding that Jesus as God with us (Emmanuel) is an understanding that Jesus is with the struggle against apartheid.[85] Loyalty for BTL is loyalty only to Jesus Christ. No racist state, no worldly power, and no human authority will triumph over "the commands of the living God."[86]

Once more, BTL understands itself as the theology which God's word necessitates. It recognizes that to be Christian means unity in a "reconciled diversity."[87] It means to "challenge racist oppression on the basis of our faith in Jesus Christ."[88] It means to "develop a critical consciousness, one which exposes the contradictions of our society." It means a commitment to struggle for liberation and the dismantling of the systemic injustice of apartheid.[89] BTL is thus a theology of the truth: an attempt to articulate "what God is saying to, and doing for the despised, the marginalized, the exploited and the oppressed."[90] Even more, it is God who energizes the struggle; because of God, the struggle exists, the struggle continues, and the struggle has come as far as it has.[91]

However, this obligation of doing BTL is only visible from a historical, sociopolitical hermeneutical reading of the Bible. I understand BTL explicitly incorporates a sociopolitical interpretation of the biblical text, which BLT claims is absent in Western historical exegesis. Thus, Mosala claims that "Jesus describes doing good in terms of service for . . . the victims of the structures of society . . . that shapes the vision of a liberated future."[92] For BTL, Jesus' cross at Calvary is not some emotional cross *all must bear*

---

83. Mofokeng, "Cross in the Search," 47.
84. Moila, "Role of Christ," 21.
85. Khabela, "Socio-Cultural Dynamics," 36.
86. Khabela, "Socio-Cultural Dynamics," 36.
87. Dwane, "Gospel and Culture," 23.
88. Goba, "Toward a Quest," 35.
89. Goba, "Toward a Quest," 35.
90. Muzorewa, "African Liberation Theology," 54.
91. Khabela, "Socio-Cultural Dynamics," 36.
92. Mosala, "Christianity and Socialism," 35–6.

but "the suffering and crucifixion of black people of South Africa."[93] Once more, to speak of God is to speak and think of the sociopolitically oppressed One. This hermeneutic sees the human experience revealed in the Bible as the predicament of oppression, inequality, and enslavement. At the same time, Jesus is the liberator of this situation of socioeconomic oppression.[94]

Mofokeng shows that the early church was socioeconomically located in a similar position as "our people" (black people in South Africa) and found the message of the Bible to be one of "survival, resistance and hope."[95] After all, it was the weak, the poor, the neglected, and the marginal people of Jesus' time who found appeal in Jesus' preaching. Or, as Mofokeng shows in another instance, Galilee's population "was suspected of racial and religious impurity. . . . Indeed Jesus came from an oppressed and exploited province in a colonized country."[96] Again, the implication is that God in Jesus of Nazareth becomes "our own flesh and blood."[97] Most people's lived experience in the biblical narrative of Palestine was one of utter poverty, "starvation, sickness, imprisonment, homelessness, separation from family and friends and persecution from authorities."[98] Interestingly enough, for BTL, there is an overwhelming opposition against hidden agendas in the book of Luke when the experiences of poverty are turned into virtues for the rich. As Mosala says: "By turning the experiences of the poor into the moral virtues of the rich, Luke has effectively eliminated the poor from his gospel."[99]

From the point that BTL is an imperative of reading the Bible with a sociopolitical hermeneutic, BTL proposes the hypothesis that black oppression during apartheid is similar to the sociopolitical oppression in the Bible. Thus, the imperative of doing BTL is also an imperative of showcasing the similarity between the biblical context and the contemporary context. At the same time, God's liberation in the biblical witness is a liberation towards the affirmation of the humanity of the oppressed.[100] Thus, for the oppressed under apartheid, to be liberated by God was also the right to

---

93. Mofokeng, "Cross in the Search," 46.
94. Moila, "Role of Christ," 15.
95. Mofokeng, "Black Christians, the Bible," 38.
96. Mofokeng, "Black Christology," 14–15.
97. Dwane, "Gospel and Culture," 22.
98. Mosala, "Black Theology," 31–32.
99. Mosala, "Black Theology," 16.
100. Mofokeng, "Cross in the Search," 44.

have power and to wield influence as an assumption of responsibility for living in the sociopolitical world of the present.[101]

Thirdly, Black Theology of Liberation understands its calling to be a theology that is explicitly public and political. Moreover, this understanding flows from the conviction that the experiences of the oppressed are essential. From such a perspective, everything is public and political.

> When a government is guilty of tyranny, when it denies human rights to some of its people, and when it commands what is forbidden by God, or forbids what God commands, then Christians may disobey or resist such a government knowing fully well what the consequences may be since governments have the power of life and death over their subjects. —MNYAMA SIZWE[102]

Ramose understands BTL's explicit nature because BTL articulates what has been implicitly preached in black churches.[103] Put another way, BTL's public and political nature is the task of scholarly expression of black preaching. BTL's first explicit public and political action is the critique of apartheid. As Muzorewa reasons, BTL reflects upon "the socio-economic, ecclesiastical and political context of the Third World peoples in Africa,"[104] not only as an act of speech but also as a call to action against the tyranny of apartheid—even if such activity is illegal and possibly fatal.[105]

Regarding the first act of BTL as public and political speech against apartheid, Mofokeng is convinced that BTL must critique the basis of capitalism (which was part and parcel of the apartheid system); "surplus extraction at the expense of workers here and abroad."[106] At the same time, BTL critiques an appropriation of the Bible, which justifies apartheid. After all, according to Mosala, it is a contradiction to include black people in God's love yet propose apartheid as an ideology "directly [derived] from the Bible."[107] Furthermore, BTL critiques the church's glorification of poverty, stating that it brings forth the endurance of misery with the hope of reward in the afterlife.[108] This critique, within the apartheid context, is public,

---

101. Mofokeng, "Cross in the Search," 45.
102. Sizwe, "Christian's Political Responsibility," 50.
103. Ramose, "Two Hands of God," 37.
104. Muzorewa, "African Liberation Theology," 53.
105. Sizwe, "Christian's Political Responsibility," 50.
106. Mofokeng, "Cross in the Search," 46.
107. Mosala, "Implications of the Text," 4.
108. Maimela, "Theological Dilemmas and Options," 19.

as the Dutch Reformed Church's theology had a significant influence on public opinion—and thus also the tolerance of poverty.

Maimela reinterprets sin, not as something personal between God and the individual but "in terms of the life of individuals who suffer injustice, oppression and destruction at the hands of their fellows."[109] Thus, political ideology and systems which "threaten[s] the life of one's fellows" are a sin against God. Once more, BTL's specific public and political task is "to challenge racist oppression on the basis of our faith in Jesus Christ."[110] It is the development of critical consciousness and the exposure of the lies of apartheid. It is a commitment to struggle and to bring an end to apartheid. Maimela goes as far as to claim that to be a Christian in apartheid South Africa means the experience of being called towards public and political involvement in the struggle against apartheid.[111]

BTL's second explicit public and political task is the public act of working towards transforming society. As Mosala states, "its task is performed in the service of a transformed and liberated social order."[112]. Lamola, in a similar vein, understands BTL as a genuinely African public endeavor in developing "African self-pride, self-reliance and service to humanity."[113] Furthermore, BTL endeavors to change the understanding of the Bible for social structures within society. Mofokeng showcases that the communism of the first church should be understood as a "tolerance of economic disparities, with the proviso that the poor should not suffer from their lack of material possessions."[114] Khabela goes as far as to state that BTL can reconcile black churches, both mainline and independent, to form an alliance with great political potential.[115]

Black Liberation

BTL's third task is the black community's real-world, sociopolitical liberation. In my opinion, two aspects can be discerned concerning this

109. Maimela, "Theological Dilemmas and Options," 21–22.
110. Goba, "Toward a Quest," 35.
111. Maimela, "Faith That Does Justice," 12.
112. Mosala, "Implications of the Text," 7.
113. Lamola, "Towards a Black Church," 9.
114. Mofokeng, "Black Christians, the Bible," 39.
115. Khabela, "Socio-Cultural Dynamics," 32.

liberation. The first is that this liberation is a witness to the Gospel. The second is that this liberation changes how society exists and operates.

> Or as the present writer likes to say, black oppressed and exploited people must liberate the gospel so that the gospel may liberate them. An enslaved gospel enslaves, a liberated gospel liberates. — Itumeleng Mosala[116]

For BTL, to work and struggle toward sociopolitical liberation is a witness to the gospel. Firstly, the nature of the gospel is under negotiation—"An enslaved gospel enslaves, a liberated gospel liberates."[117] Whereas a breakaway from the enslaving gospel of Western Christianity is summarily rejected (by Western Christianity) because there is no salvation outside the church, BTL opens a space for negotiation both within the mainline churches and for independent churches.[118]

Moreover, BTL points to how the gospel has been corrupted through the phenomenon that oppression is routine precisely because the gospel's imperatives for sociopolitical liberation and reconciliation have been ignored and ineffective.[119] That being said, for BTL, where God stands is essential. It is only through God's mercy, salvation, and choice to and for the marginalized that all people receive mercy, salvation, and are chosen.[120]

From this negotiation, Mofokeng speaks of the struggle for liberation as a witness to "the victorious presence of Jesus Christ."[121] Maimela is convinced that the gospel is "the promotion of justice, peace and reconciliation in society," and our calling is to "make the Kingdom of God more visible and present . . . through the social structures [we] create."[122] In the context of BTL, the "cause of Jesus Christ [is equal] with the cause of social and political revolution."[123] In this understanding, faith is an active force of resistance against unjust structures and people, and in the apartheid context, resistance against the "oppression of blacks." At the same time, as Mosala opines, socialist politics and the structuring of society through a socialist

---

116. Mosala, "Black Theology," 39.
117. Mosala, "Black Theology," 39.
118. Lamola, "Towards a Black Church," 8.
119. Maimela, "Theological Dilemmas and Options," 17.
120. Mofokeng, "Cross in the Search," 48.
121. Mofokeng, "Black Christology," 9.
122. Maimela, "Theological Dilemmas and Options," 25.
123. Moila, "Role of Christ," 22.

ideology are part and parcel of the biblical witness, especially as interpreted by the progressive Christian traditions.[124] Even more, capitalism, as existing in apartheid, is against the gospel. Muzorewa agrees with this sentiment, proclaiming: "Christ came to save! Suffering cannot continue when God in Christ steps into the situation to save the creature!"[125] Furthermore, peace is vital for BTL, and "peace is the active presence of justice, the well-being of all."[126]

Thus, black liberation is a pursuit of changing the operation and nature of society:

> [Black South Africans are] committed to reordering the state in order to establish a just society. Indeed, black South Africans do not see white South Africans as enemies to be eliminated, but as fellow citizens who need a change of heart. Moreover, black South Africans want a non-racial society, and do not believe that the state is a product of social conflict and violence.[127]

For BTL, to work and struggle for sociopolitical liberation is the concrete pursuit of changing apartheid society towards a non-racial society that is inclusive of all people.[128] Khabela warns that reconciliation has too often meant that black people must suffer and give themselves up for the sake of others instead of leading toward liberation. Christian reconciliation between black and white in South Africa should mean "political, social and economic justice."[129] For Mofokeng black culture is a culture of "subversive protest against material, political and social dehumanization of black people" which has been incorporated into the very fabric of BTL.[130] In such a sense, black culture is actively working towards the complete liberation of the black experience.

Mosala takes a robust oppositional stance against capitalism while reminding us that apartheid is a capitalist system. "[The] content of the goal of BTL is to be struggled for from the totalizing hold of modern capitalism."[131] Furthermore, economic liberation is also a land issue. Ramose suggests that

---

124. Mosala, "Christianity and Socialism," 30.
125. Muzorewa, "African Liberation Theology," 54.
126. Khabela, "Socio-Cultural Dynamics," 37.
127. Ngcokovane, "Ethical Problems, Options and Strategies," 32.
128. Ngcokovane, "Ethical Problems, Options and Strategies," 32.
129. Khabela, "Socio-Cultural Dynamics," 37.
130. Mofokeng, "Black Christology," 9.
131. Mosala, "Black Theology," 34.

land is essential to all human life, and thus inclusive land reform is fundamental to liberation in South Africa.[132]

BTL is aware of the trapping of independence without liberation, stating clearly that "a progressive economic system" needs to be set up. Mosala goes as far as to state that capitalism is no option for liberation, indeed if "we do not go socialist we can only go barbaric."[133] Thus, Mosala claims that "the content of the goal of BTL is to be struggled for from the totalizing hold of modern capitalism."[134]

Black Theology of Liberation since Democracy

There can be no question that Black Theology of Liberation (BTL) took a hiatus when South Africa became a democracy in 1994.[135] This was because the most prolific academics in BTL: "Itumeleng Mosala, Takatso Mofokeng, Simon Maimela, Smangaliso Mkhatswa, Frank Chikane and others ... [became] all manner of administrators and state functionaries."[136] At the same time, I believe South Africa experienced euphoria with the emergence of democracy, which proponents of BTL were merely unable to circumvent in contextual analyses of the new situation.

To adequately propose the position of BTL since democracy in South Africa, I offer the following three markers.[137] First, BTL, since democracy endeavors to integrate with African Theology[138] and African Independent Churches (AICs). Second, since democracy, BTL has reemphasized its tasks of contextualization and biblical hermeneutics. Third, since democracy, BTL has become deeply aware of the agency of Africans.

---

132. Ramose, "Two Hands of God," 30.
133. Mosala, "Christianity and Socialism," 29–30.
134. Mosala, "Christianity and Socialism," 34.
135. Molobi, "Past and Future of Black Theology," 2.
136. Maluleke, "Black and African Theology," 194.
137. Taking note that these markers are reductionistic and that these markers are by no means understood and researched homogeneously.
138. I take African Theology to mean theological thoughts of African Indigenous Religion.

Integration of Black Theology of Liberation with African Theology and AICs

Molobi and Saayman opine that democracy in South Africa brought with it the need for a new alignment of purpose for African theological thought—as an integration of BTL, African Theology, and the theologies of AICs.[139] At the time of writing, they discerned a lacuna with regards to focal images for mission in Africa, even though there were calls for contemplation on "endemic violence, the collapse of black family life, the abuse of women and children ... [and] poverty and HIV/Aids." Furthermore, according to Molobi and Saayman, the differences between African Theologians, Black Theologians, and AICs started to dissipate in the late 1980s with the rise of "issues such as neo-colonialism, corrupt leadership, and the oppression of indigenous voices of protest."[140] West opines that all African Theologies, including BTL, African theology, and the theology of AICs, are liberation theologies.[141] Thus, no longer could African Theologians be concerned only with the renewal of African indigenous culture and religion. Neither could Black Theologians focus solely on liberation. At the same time, a less "schizophrenic relationship" between African culture and Christianity had emerged, giving way to more nuanced "translatability" of Christianity within the African context.[142]

Molobi and Saayman, in consideration of the realities mentioned above, propose three focal areas for integrating BTL, African theology, and AICs in democratic South Africa: Liberation, Ecclesiology, and Christology.[143]

> Suddenly, not everything smells of roses, because in many African countries repression and endemic corruption are still the rule rather than the exception. —VICTOR MOLOBI AND WILLEM SAAYMAN[144]

The point being made by Molobi and Saayman seems to me to be: although colonization (and apartheid) is historically over, it is still everywhere, in new forms, and liberation still evades the structures of South

---

139. Molobi and Saayman, "Time for Complementarity," 327.
140. Molobi and Saayman, "Time for Complementarity," 330.
141. West, *Stolen Bible*, 354.
142. Maluleke, "Black and African Theology," 203.
143. Molobi and Saayman, "Time for Complementarity," 332–35.
144. Molobi and Saayman, "Time for Complementarity," 332.

Africa. Ndlovu-Gatsheni calls this Coloniality "an invisible power structure that sustains colonial relations of exploitation and domination long after the end of direct colonialism."[145] Thus, neither African theology nor AICs can ignore the need for Africans to obtain and experience liberation in its fullness. At the same time, BTL can no longer be convinced that liberation is merely political liberation. Thus, Molobi and Saayman propose a holistic liberation, whereby Jesus of Nazareth inaugurated a new and liberating community differing greatly from the earthly systemic structures of oppression, which still exist in the democratic context of South Africa.[146]

Maluleke shows that other theologians have explicitly chosen to replace the concept of *liberation*.[147] Jesse Mugambi instead speaks about reconstruction and includes the inculturation of African theology therein. Charles Villa-Vicencio speaks about critical solidarity with the democratic powers. At the same time, however, there are definite voices of critique against the abuses of the new elites in South Africa.[148]

For Vuyani Vellem and Allan Boesak, reconstruction and development cannot occur without liberation. Vellem proposes that liberation must be "the framework within which reconstruction and development" occur.[149] Boesak showcases how liberation is still absent in the democratic context, claiming that the struggle after democratization has merely evolved into more magnificent beasts, "into global struggles, against new forms of global apartheid, new and renewed struggles for justice."[150] He specifies four areas of struggle for liberation: the poor and their ability to live in the contextual realities. Second, human sexuality and gender justice. Third, pluralism and its implications. And fourth, globalization and the influence it has on all of life. I will get to the idea of the importance of the agency of the marginalized for BTL a bit later; yet, as Maluleke and Nadar show, some theological reflections have proposed that liberation is only possible when the oppressed are the agents of liberation.[151]

---

145. Ndlovu-Gatsheni, "Coloniality of Power," 48.

146. Molobi and Saayman, "Time for Complementarity," 332.

147. Maluleke, "Black and African Theology," 204.

148. See Maluleke, "Black and African Theology"; de Wet and Kruger, "Blessed Are Those That Hunger"; Wepener and Pieterse, "Angry Preaching."

149. Vellem, "Symbol of Liberation," 131.

150. Boesak, "'Hope Unprepared to Accept Things,'" 1057.

151. Maluleke and Nadar, "Alien Fraudsters," 8.

Postcolonial Homiletics?

An essential contribution to Black Theology of Liberation in partnership with African theology and AICs since democracy is the simultaneous critique of Western forms of ecclesiology and the possibilities of new ecclesiologies.

> In the first place, the church in Africa must experience the presence of God not through documents and traditions, but through the existential communal realities marking the rhythm of natural life: birth and death, sowing and harvesting, thunderstorms and road accidents, celebrations and mourning. —Victor Molobi and Willem Saayman[152]

> We argue first that the more there is change, the more things stay the same. Stated otherwise, we argue that if there is democratic dispensation in South Africa, it is more likely that the church stays the same. —Vuyani Vellem[153]

Molobi and Saayman propose Western ecclesiologies are "basically ecclesiologies without any missiology."[154] Their counterproposal calls for an understanding of the church in the African context as "the disfigured body of Christ," which takes seriously the economic injustices which have historically caused (and still cause) "poverty, hunger, unemployment, and disease." Thus, an authentically African ecclesiology will practice theology from the position of existential realities within the African context.[155] Vuyani Vellem interprets the church within democracy as the church in apartheid.[156] With this, he means that the church is shackled by a "colonial legacy" as "an instrument of cultural dominance" and "compla[cent] with a life-killing capitalist exploitation."[157] To counter these realities of a church that has stayed the same, Vellem proposes the church as "the Church of the Struggle." In this line of thought, "the church in South Africa is the black poor person's lived experience," and from the perspective of the poor in South Africa, struggle is a daily existential reality. Moreover, what Vellem foundationally calls for is an unshackling of method, of combining classical understandings of the church with the lived experience of struggle: "the

---

152. Molobi and Saayman, "Time for Complementarity," 334.
153. Vellem, "Unshackling the Church," 2.
154. Molobi and Saayman, "Time for Complementarity," 333.
155. Molobi and Saayman, "Time for Complementarity," 334.
156. Vellem, "Unshackling the Church," 2.
157. Vellem, "Unshackling the Church," 5.

subversive character of the church is in the memory of the miserable, the condition of blackness."

However, in Molobi and Saayman's understanding,

> The AICs can make a valuable contribution here, primarily as they already exist as African ecclesiastical institutions free from Western apron and purse strings. The structured theological reflection on important issues such as inculturation, Christology, etc, which has already been undertaken by African Theologians is of equal importance. Also, the strong emphasis among Black Theologians on analysis of the social, political and economic contexts within which the African church must carry out its mission is of equal importance.[158]

The third aspect of integrating Black Theology of Liberation, African theology, and AICs is the call for a Christology which takes seriously African Christians' existential questions.

> Christianization can therefore no longer be equated with westernization, and the white Christ of mission history has to be replaced by the black Christ of Africa. —VICTOR MOLOBI AND WILLEM SAAYMAN[159]

Molobi and Saayman are very critical concerning how Christ was introduced in South Africa by colonial missionaries and theologians, claiming that questions and matters of Christology have been proposed by them which are irrelevant to the African experience. Inculturation of African culture and dignity must occur within a genuinely African Christology, which Molobi and Saayman are convinced is possible through the convergence of BTL, African theology, and the theology of AICs, especially in relating Christ to the understanding of ancestors.[160] The missiological knowledge of Jesus as the cosmic Christ, the head and beginning of the cosmos, should aid in describing the universal presence of the ancestors as the "guardians of life in Africa."

An exciting proposal for Christology in South Africa comes from Tinyiko Maluleke, who (according to Urbaniak) "locates Jesus' body in the bodies of his fellow Africans."[161] Maluleke argues regarding Christology

---

158. Molobi and Saayman, "Time for Complementarity," 334.
159. Molobi and Saayman, "Time for Complementarity," 334.
160. Molobi and Saayman, "Time for Complementarity," 335.
161. Urbaniak, "Between the Christ of Deep Incarnation," 180.

that the Western understanding has been centered on talking about Jesus as "Christ."[162] According to this case, the title of Christ locates Jesus at the right hand of God. In contrast, Jesus of Nazareth is located as walking "the streets of Tyre, Sydon, Galilea, and Jericho." Christ calls for worship and adoration, while the Jesus of the streets is human, crying at the sign of losing his friend Lazarus. Maluleke goes on to say that African Christology is still developing; however, in my reading of him, I am convinced that he wants to privilege a Christology which is interested in the social location of Jesus of Nazareth for the African context. Maluleke proposes that an understanding of Christology is already being "enacted" in Africa. AICs are already vocalizing their experience of Christ in healing ceremonies. BTL and African theology are theologizing about Christ as "healer, the Black Messiah, the ancestor, the elder brother, the crucified one and the master of initiation."[163]

Furthermore, as Urbaniak proposes, Maluleke's African Jesus is a Jesus "with unresolved issues."[164] A Jesus who suffers as African people suffer, albeit the Healer; this Jesus does not offer answers but suffers alongside the African poor; even more, he endures as the African poor. As Maluleke suggests, African theologians "have noted the emphasis on the crucified and suffering Christ as opposed to the risen and victorious Christ."[165] This has brought with it a Christology of tragedy, where joy is experienced amidst pain and strength in suffering, for "Christ appears daily in war-torn African villages . . . resides in the squalid slum-cities of Africa . . . [and] is being crucified in the emaciated and flea-ridden bodies of Africa's starving, dying children."[166] At the same time, however, Maluleke reasons that the "identification with Jesus is never total." There is always an apparent otherness of Jesus, even within the oneness and identification with Africans.[167] In an exciting turn of events, this understanding that human beings cannot be like Christ in fullness has given African women leverage against the dominance of patriarchal structures in Africa. Once again, Maluleke is persistent in reiterating, this time from the thoughts of Desmond Tutu, that "God's image and glory resided in and was reflected on all the despised, exploited and

162. Maluleke, "Christ in Africa," 57.
163. Maluleke, "Christ in Africa," 62.
164. Urbaniak, "Between the Christ of Deep Incarnation," 134.
165. Maluleke, "Crucified Reflected," 84.
166. Maluleke, "Crucified Reflected," 83–84.
167. Maluleke, "Crucified Reflected," 86.

suffering people [during apartheid]." My interpretation hereof is a simultaneous dialectical understanding: Jesus is the African poor, and Jesus is utterly other than the African poor: Jesus is the wholly Other and reflected in the eyes of the Africans who suffer.[168]

Biblical and Contextual Hermeneutics

> This choice of interlocutors is more than an ethical commitment, it is also an epistemological commitment, requiring an interpretive starting point within the social experience and social analysis of the poor and marginalized themselves. —GERALD WEST[169]

Maluleke believes that the most longstanding influence of BTL is its biblical hermeneutics.[170] According to West, BTL's critical contextualization and biblical hermeneutics stem from its interlocutors: those whom God has preferentially chosen as interlocutors: the marginalized, the poor, and the poor subaltern.[171] However, Vuyani Vellem shows that BTL's interlocution changed after democracy. Because of the black church's critical solidarity with the governing party (African National Congress) after 1994, Vellem proposes that the interlocutors for this "critical solidarity" became "a black middle class person rather than the poor non-person."[172] Vellem shows that losing the nonperson as interlocutor implies "the poor are left alone." Thus, the struggle of the subaltern is ignored, and the struggle moves to other spaces. In other words, with the loss of BTL's interlocutor in democratic South Africa, the authenticity and viability of BTL should be under scrutiny.

Allan Boesak, however, argues that the nonperson is still the interlocutor for the hermeneutics of BTL.[173] He proposes, therefore, that BTL

---

168. Emmanuel Katongole, although not a South African theologian, has a different take on the association between God and those who suffer. Taking the African-American religious expression as an example, he shows that the slaves identified their "own suffering with Christ's forsakenness on the cross" (Katongole, *Born from Lament*, 114). And through this identification, they found strength and hope in active resistance to the injustices experienced. Katongole, in my opinion, represents a perspective not from where God is, but from the lived experience of the subaltern. This implies further that the subaltern takes upon herself the responsibility to identify with the suffering (of) Christ.

169. West, *Stolen Bible*, 354.

170. Maluleke, "Black and African Theology," 206.

171. West, *Stolen Bible*, 353–54.

172. Vellem, "Interlocution and Black Theology," 4.

173. Boesak, "Hope Unprepared to Accept Things," 1056.

is "the prophetic witness" and "theology at the edge." For Boesak, BTL in democracy tries not to be relevant but instead gives the necessary tools to reflect "intellectually and with integrity on the people's struggles . . . it means [that] we are informed."[174]

In my contemplation on Boesak, I am convinced that Boesak is the utmost proponent of BTL which theologizes in the same manner now as during apartheid.[175] I have proposed that Boesak's simultaneous understanding is that the "Bible has specific sociopolitical relevance" in the current context and that the evil of the context should be named explicitly.[176]

On the one hand, Boesak underscores BTL's contextual and biblical hermeneutics. Still, this position implicitly underscores the hermeneutical superiority of colonial theological thought. Vellem believes this repeating BTL practiced during apartheid "takes the gains of the school [of BTL] backwards."[177] Irrelevant to the implication of this tradition of BTL, others are convinced of the necessity of acute, intense, and accurate contextualization as the tradition of BTL during apartheid dictates.[178]

Maluleke opines that there is no consensus on the question of which hermeneutics is most appropriate and liberating for Africans in the context of democratic South Africa. However, it has become clear that African theologians cannot pretend "that the Bible, the gospel or the 'Christian faith' interprets itself" and that things go wrong only when misinterpretations of the Bible occur.[179] At a conservative estimate, the implication hereof is that hermeneutical innocence is not at all a possibility for the future of BTL. Viewing it from the perspective of a liberal evaluation, the future of Black Theological hermeneutics will turn to sources other than the Bible for the liberation of Africans.

---

174. Boesak, "'Hope Unprepared to Accept Things,'" 1057.

175. This being said, Allan Boesak by no means has the same influence as he had in the '80s and '90s. Today, his voice is constrained to academic spaces, not because of a new strategy, but merely because he does not have the public platform he had during apartheid. Moreover, his political career within the ANC may have forced him to return to the fundamentals of BTL as practices during apartheid. In a very real sense, he became disillusioned with the realpolitik of the ANC (see Boesak, *Running with Horses*).

176. Wessels, "Contemplating Allan Boesak's Fascination," 203.

177. Vellem, "Un-Thinking the West," 1.

178. Manala, "'Better Life for All'"; Wessels, "Contemplating Allan Boesak's Fascination."

179. Maluleke, "Black and African Theology," 206.

Comparison between (BTL) & Postcolonial Thought

An exciting development for BTL is the movement away from portraying the poor as helpless victims. Maluleke shows a movement towards an understanding that the poor are active agents who, in a myriad of ways, politically, economically, and spiritually, have participated (and continuously participated) in life.[180]

The Agency of Africans

> Behind most notions of agency is the basic suggestion that human beings, even the most oppressed, marginalized and seemingly destitute among them, have the potential, possibility and even ability to act as (moral) agents of transformation and change in their own lives and in the lives of others. —TINYIKO MALULEKE AND SAROJINI NADAR[181]

Maluleke claims that BTL, since democracy (and post-Cold War), has ceased to interpret "the poor as conned and helpless victims needing to be roused from their slumber."[182] Instead, there has been a movement towards discovering, exploring and interpreting the agency of the African poor respectfully. As Maluleke and Nadar aptly state, there has never been a doubt about the agency of people from the upper and middle classes, as well as whites.[183] Now BTL has awoken to the agentic potential of the poor, marginalized, and subaltern.

For Maluleke, all emerging schools of BTL after apartheid are, in one way or another, "a rediscovery of the agency of African Christians in the face of great odds."[184] Molobi and Saayman are convinced that the agency of Africans has always been present, even during the colonial missions.[185] They opine that Africans were never just objects without agency but always subjects exercising their agency, albeit in subversive ways. Maluleke and Nadar articulate the discourse on agency thoroughly in their contemplation. For them, the "most wretched victims of oppression" have found ways of survival even if these tactics of survival seem ineffective to outside observers; even more, it is often the academic observer who is at fault for

---

180. Maluleke, "Black and African Theology," 205.
181. Maluleke and Nadar, "Alien Fraudsters," 7–8.
182. Maluleke, "Black and African Theology," 205.
183. Maluleke and Nadar, "Alien Fraudsters," 6–7.
184. Maluleke, "Black and African Theology," 207.
185. Molobi and Saayman, "Time for Complementarity," 328.

misapprehending the techniques of agency.[186] Furthermore, the "idea that the oppressors [can] have total control over the potential, desires, and direction of the oppressed ought to be radically modified if not abandoned altogether."[187]

Maluleke and Nadar's exciting contribution to the agency discourse is their caution about who conducts the conversation. They show that the current discussion on agency is driven mainly by white men, which leads them to propose that the function of the agency discourse may be "exclusion and control."[188] Since white men (academics) are the most removed from the existential realities of the interlocutor as marginalized people, the danger is paramount of creating "an imaginary agent interlocutor in some imaginary South African township."[189] At the same time, however, Maluleke and Nadar are not ignorant of the positional problems of black and women academics regarding the agency discourse.

POSTCOLONIAL THEORY—GENEALOGICAL OVERVIEW

In this second part of the chapter, I will contemplate postcolonial theory. Unlike BTL, my contemplation on postcolonial theory will not be localized to South Africa. Thus, there is no localized historical moment of disruption, not to say there aren't different schools of thought. My original plan was to focus exclusively on African postcolonial scholars. However, I have decided to include international scholars because I thought it would aid in the quality and comprehensiveness of this book. I have thus decided to expand this genealogical overview of postcolonial thought to be more global.

---

186. Maluleke and Nadar, "Alien Fraudsters," 8.

187. Maluleke and Nadar, "Alien Fraudsters," 8.

188. Maluleke and Nadar, "Alien Fraudsters," 7.

189. Conversely, I have much appreciation for Johan Cilliers, "Worshipping in the Townships." He converses adequately with the likes of Abraham Berinyuu and Gabriel Setiloane. I agree with Cilliers' proposal that the space of worship in the township is a liminal space, although I would opt for a space of negotiation. However, I disagree with Cilliers that the three keywords of township worship are: "anti-structural (prophecy), new community (communitas), and possibility (imagination)" (p. 81). Prophecy, communitas, and imagination can be associated with any place of worship. However, in conversation with Vellem, "Cracking the Eurocentric Code," 277. I would contend that *liberation* should at least encompass Cilliers' keywords, and therefore *struggle*—economic and political—is quintessential to worship in the townships.

However, some constraints will still stand. Only postcolonial scholars who have written in English (or whose work has been translated into English) will be considered. At the same time, I must make choices of focal images because the study cannot adequately contemplate every aspect of the sources to the full.

Thus, I have made three choices. Firstly, I will focus on the following postcolonial scholars as primary sources (with the knowledge that some of these scholars choose to speak about decoloniality instead of postcolonial[190]): Homi Bhabha, Ngũgĩ wa Thiong'o, Emmanuel Lartey, Frantz Fanon, Walter Mignolo, Steve Biko, Aimé Césaire, and Achille Mbembe. The second choice is a choice of focal images.

I have delimited three themes in postcolonial thought, which I will use as focal images for a genealogical overview of postcolonial thought. These are 1) the irrational myth and the decolonization of the mind; 2) moving of the center; and 3) a decentered, fragmented identity. The third choice is to seriously consider Walter Mignolo's proposal that the postcolonial "struggle is for changing the *terms* in addition to the *content* of the conversation."[191] Thus, I will consider how the terms and content interplay within the three focal images throughout my contemplation of postcolonial thought.

The Irrational Myth and the Decolonization of the Mind

> De-coloniality, then, means working toward a vision of human life that is not dependent upon or structured by the forced imposition of one ideal of society over those that differ, which is what modernity/coloniality does and, hence, where decolonization of the mind should begin. The struggle is for changing the terms in addition to the content of the conversation. —WALTER MIGNOLO[192]

Postcolonial thought's first task is naming and deconstructing the irrational myth of colonialism in all forms, as historical colonialism, but also

---

190. The differences between postcolonial and decoloniality have been touched upon in the first chapter. I think that these differences, albeit nuanced, are outside of the scope of consideration for this book. I will thus consider them as different schools of thought within Postcolonial Theory and borrow with due consideration of differences.

191. Mignolo, "Delinking," 459 (my italics). My preliminary intuition about the difference between BTL and postcolonial thought is that BTL has been accurate in changing the content of the conversation but lacks in changing the terms of the conversation.

192. Mignolo, "Delinking," 459.

as modernity and the (neo)colonialism[193] intertwined in contemporary democratic capitalism.

Postcolonial scholars insist on thoroughly naming, unveiling, and deconstructing (neo)colonialism. This task is a critical reading of the context of what Mignolo calls the "irrational myth" of (neo)colonialism.[194] Mignolo shows a spell at work, where neo-liberalism, modernity, and democracy are promoted as the all-encompassing solution and salvation to life's problems.[195] Yet, simultaneously, in the interest of expanding this myth (and this is where the myth becomes irrational), there is "justification for genocidal violence."[196] This means that colonialism brings forth wounding of those on the receiving side of the irrational myth. It is "wretchedness, emptiness, squalor created by Eurocentric colonialism and apartheid."[197] Vellem proposes that colonial logic chooses elimination instead of persuasion.[198]

Moreover, this irrational myth is entirely present in all colonial logics of salvation, whether "Christianity, civilization, modernization, and development after WWII or market democracy after the fall of the Soviet Union."[199] Thus, any structure which imposes "one ideal of society over those that differ" is the irrational myth of colonization.[200] From a contemporary context, wherein Brexit and Trump are realities, Vellem includes imperialism, racism, and neofascism as colonial logic. For him, the emergence of Brexit and Trump showcases a manifestation of (neo)colonialism in narcissistic form, aided by "psychological and ideological confusion."[201]

Moreover, in the South African context, there has existed, and still exists, sympathy with the core values of racism, which has led to a democratic government reimposing trauma and violence on black people, as far

---

193. I use brackets with (neo)colonialism to indicate the porous nature of the coloniality of the past. The newness of (neo)colonialism is not that new and the break with the colonial past is not that clear-cut. See Hook, *(Post)Apartheid Conditions*, 5, for more on the idea that the present realities are not definitive breaks with the past.

194. Mignolo, "Delinking," 454. Others have coined this the "colonial abyss" (An Yountae) and the "colonial death project" (Julia Suárez-Krabbe)—quoted from Ndlovu-Gatsheni, *Epistemic Freedom in Africa*, 75.

195. Mignolo, "Delinking," 450.

196. Mignolo, "Delinking," 454.

197. Vellem, "Un-Thinking the West," 2.

198. Vellem, "Un-Thinking the West," 7.

199. Mignolo, "Delinking," 463–64.

200. Mignolo, "Delinking," 459.

201. Vellem, "Un-Thinking the West," 3.

as Vellem is concerned.[202] Even after apartheid and in the new democratic dispensation, black people are still "an oppressed and suffering group of people . . . coping and dealing with the scars of white oppression." Notwithstanding emancipation projects (i.e., the struggle against apartheid). Still, global, imperial, and colonizing logics enjoy epistemological privilege. The new historical decolonial dispensations repeat the violence of colonialism.[203] Frantz Fanon is even more pronounced in his judgment of new governmental powers after emancipation, claiming: "[The] Spoiled children of yesterday's colonialism and today's governing powers, they oversee the looting of the few national resources. . . . Their doctrine is to proclaim the absolute need for nationalizing the theft of the nation."[204]

Another important unveiling in postcolonial thought is the unveiling of Christianity's part in colonization. Vuyani Vellem shows that the Christian understanding of creation out of nothing brought with it the dual understanding that "black people were reduced to nothingness [and] white people [were upheld] as creators."[205] Fanon equates Christianity with pesticides, claiming that Christianity understood its part in colonization as the rooting out of all forms of existence, knowledge, and practices interpreted from a Western perspective as "heresy, natural impulses, and evil."[206] He goes on: "The Church in the colonies is the white man's Church, a foreigners' Church. . . . It does not call the colonized to the ways of God, but to the ways of the white man, to the ways of the master, the ways of the oppressor."[207]

Similarly, Ishmael Tetteh shows how Catholic and Protestant Christian mission forcibly attacked African culture and religion in the past and has recently been taken up by Pentecostal and Charismatic Christian movements.[208] Even African languages were incorporated into this attack on African culture by Christianity. Ngũgĩ wa Thiong'o shows that African stories were colonized to carry a moral message with the implication of "revealing the unerring finger of a white God in human affairs."[209]

---

202. Vellem, "Un-Thinking the West," 5.
203. Mignolo, "Delinking," 459.
204. Fanon, *Wretched of the Earth*, 12.
205. Vellem, "Un-Thinking the West," 8.
206. Fanon, *Wretched of the Earth*, 6.
207. Fanon, *Wretched of the Earth*, 6–7.
208. Tetteh, *Inspired African Mystical Gospel*, 25.
209. Wa Thiong'o, *Decolonising the Mind*, 67.

I want to return once more to postcolonial thinkers' unveiling of the violence of coloniality. Mbembe believes colonial violence is threefold.[210] First, it is the founding violence of justifying conquest, both in creating its right to conquer and denying the right of those captured. Secondly, coloniality created its own authority, thereby "converting the founding violence into authorizing authority." Thirdly, it is violence that maintains, spreads, and makes permanent the authority of coloniality. This final violence is appropriated through imagination, creating the illusion that society cannot exist without coloniality. The first violence can be described as military conquest, and the second as a political dictatorship. However, the third violence is defined by Ngũgĩ wa Thiong'o as the domination of "the mental universe of the colonized, the control, through culture, of how people perceive themselves and their relationship to the world."[211]

Another aspect of the third form of violence is the superiority of Western values. Not only are Western values understood and proposed as superior, but they are enforced with such violence until the colonized "have proclaimed loud and clear that white values reign supreme."[212] Furthermore, the violence of colonizing the imagination and mind is reinforced in colonial education. As Ngũgĩ wa Thiong'o states, colonial education works against the possibilities of creating confidence and mastery in overcoming life's obstacles but rather "make[s] them feel their inadequacies, their weaknesses and their incapacities in the face of reality."[213] Put another way, colonial education binds the agency of the colonized, making people unable to participate actively in their futures.

In a concluding unveiling of the irrational myth of colonization, Mbembe shows how the body of "the stranger" and the recognition that their body is like mine is a problem for "Western consciousness."[214] The foundations of Western knowledge are both limiting and dangerous. And the antidote is a call to stand for "border epistemology,"[215] the decoloniza-

---

210. Mbembe, *On the Postcolony*, 25.
211. Wa Thiong'o, *Decolonising the Mind*, 16.
212. Fanon, *Wretched of the Earth*, 8.
213. Wa Thiong'o, *Decolonising the Mind*, 56.
214. Mbembe, *On the Postcolony*, 2.
215. Mignolo, "Delinking," 455.

tion of the mind,[216] and an understanding of development which enriches workers' consciousness.[217]

Or, as Mignolo so eloquently states, there should be an "affirming [of] the modes and principles of knowledge that have been denied by the rhetoric of Christianization, civilization, progress, development, [and] market democracy."[218]

On the Postcolony

Before turning to the call of decolonization of the mind, there should be due consideration and contemplation on the postcolony; that is to say, how politics in the postcolony showcases itself after political liberation.

> "And what should the book be about?" I asked Max [du Preez]. "About the people that Zuma surrounds himself with. The Shauns and the Mdlulis and the Ntlemezas and the Jibas and the Nhlekos and the Hlaudis and the Zwanes. But also about the faceless, nameless bunch behind them that play a vital role to keep him in power." "And out of prison," I added. "Precisely," he said. "And don't forget that they also enable him and the family to make money," I said. "Just think about his son's links to the Guptas and illegal tobacco smugglers." —JACQUES PAUW[219]

In Jacques Pauw's 2017 book, *The President's Keepers*, Pauw has a conversation with Max du Preez about the book's writing. In the South African context, where the conversation takes place, South Africa is a country that has had over twenty years of freedom and democracy. However, the then-president, Jacob Zuma, administrated his presidency so that he, his family, and his friends could benefit through corruption. In a recent news article, Mashele claimed that the current president, Cyril Ramaphosa, has continued on a similar trend, albeit not as publicly scandalous. Mashele continues:

> As for the poor and the unemployed, the waiting continues. They see on television men and women dressed in suits, gathered in much-vaunted investment jamborees that promise to grow the economy and create jobs. While the poor and the unemployed

216. Wa Thiong'o, *Decolonising the Mind*, 108.
217. Fanon, *Wretched of the Earth*, 141.
218. Mignolo, "Delinking," 463.
219. Pauw, *President's Keepers*, 22.

don't understand economics, they know that investment conferences are meaningless to them, for they have never seen one job coming to their village or township because of a meeting held in Sandton.[220]

This brings forth a nagging question about the inability of the "postcolony" to become what it has envisioned itself to be: a place of liberation and prosperity. This is, as the postcolony has seemingly been liberated from the colonial powers of yesteryear. Put another way, why does democratic South Africa so closely reflect the power abuses to the benefit of the few as in colonial times? Why has the struggle against apartheid not brought forth the dreams and hopes of the Freedom Charter?

As Achille Mbembe shows, there is a façade in the postcolony at work, where the newly elected leaders, often of one overwhelmingly majority party, find ways of repressing dissidents.[221] The governing party becomes society, whatever benefits the party, and the president becomes "state legitimacy." Frantz Fanon is far less reserved with his judgment of such a situation. He calls the newly elected governing powers "spoiled children of yesterday's colonialism," claiming that they are only interested in preaching nationalization to steal the national resources for themselves.[222]

It is important to note that liberation is not merely one struggle, that of political and economic decolonization, but also "epistemological decolonization."[223] Let me turn to the call for the decolonization of the mind.

Decolonization of the Mind

After the deconstruction of the irrational myth of (neo)colonization, postcolonial thought calls for the decolonization of the mind.

> Decolonization of knowledge shall be understood in the constant double movement of unveiling the geo-political location of theology, secular philosophy and scientific reason and simultaneously affirming the modes and principles of knowledge that have been

---

220. Mashele, "Ramaphosa Bankrupting State."
221. Mbembe, *On the Postcolony*, 105.
222. Fanon, *Wretched of the Earth*, 12.
223. Mignolo, "Delinking," 454.

denied by the rhetoric of Christianization, civilization, progress, development, [and] market democracy. —WALTER MIGNOLO[224]

As Mignolo shows, there is no linear movement of deconstruction and unveiling and then the decolonization of the mind. Instead, this is a constant circle of decolonizing the mind, maybe even the postcolonial circle. Mignolo's understanding of the decolonization of the mind is the affirmation of "modes and principles of knowledge" denied by the colonial way of thinking. Once more, decolonization and postcolonial thought go further. An awareness of the need for political and economic liberation, as well as epistemological decolonization, exists. Liberation is only complete if both are present.[225] There is the need for a "delinking that leads to decolonial epistemic shift and brings to the foreground other epistemologies, other principles of knowledge and understanding and, consequently, other economy [sic], other politics, other ethics."[226]

Vuyani Vellem uses the isiXhosa word *Umoya* (meaning wind, breath, and spirit) to convey his understanding of the decolonization of the mind.[227] He understands the current (neo)colonial context to be one of "breathlessness." Still, with the Umoya, the breath of God comes into play, raising the spirit of the black person to "reject the finality of the West." In a similar movement as what I deem the postcolonial circle, Vellem's Umoja rejects history, politics, and economics skewed in favor of Europe and calls for acknowledging the agency of Black Africans, both in history and in the present. No more will Black Africans be seen as "pathological objects of the periodization of the West."

Ngũgĩ wa Thiong'o shows that political and economic colonization is impossible without "mental control."[228] Thus, there was complete subjugation of the culture of the colonized, "their art, dances, religions, history, geography, education, orature and literature." And on the other hand, an elevation of the colonizer's culture and language. "The domination of a people's language by the languages of the colonizing nations was crucial to the domination of the mental universe of the colonized." Therefore, the breakage of colonization is only possible once this lingual colonization and

---

224. Mignolo, "Delinking," 463.
225. Mignolo, "Delinking," 454.
226. Mignolo, "Delinking," 453.
227. Vellem, "Un-Thinking the West," 8.
228. Wa Thiong'o, *Decolonising the Mind*, 16.

the concomitant disassociation from "the immediate environment."[229] is broken and the mind is liberated from it. However, in my reading of Ngũgĩ wa Thiong'o, I do not believe he calls for a specific language to replace English (as an example of a colonial language). What he calls for instead is "the rediscovery of the real language of humankind: the language of struggle."[230]

The language of struggle, to my mind, strongly resonates with BTL during the apartheid years and the ideas that the black experience should be the hermeneutical starting point, reading the Bible with an eye for the liberation of black people, and constructing a public and political struggle for liberation.[231]

Steve Biko's interpretation of the colonization of the mind is just as chilling. When he speaks about the colonization of the mind, he calls it "spiritual poverty" and asks this about the black person in South Africa:

> What makes the black man fail to tick? Is he convinced of his own accord of his inabilities? Does he lack in his genetic make-up that rare quality that makes a man willing to die for the realization of his aspirations? Or is he simply a defeated person? The answer to this is not a clearcut one. It is, however, nearer to the last suggestion than anything else.[232]

If the black person under apartheid, and still in democratic South Africa,[233] is spiritually (and consciously) defeated, Steve Biko's proposal of what a decolonized mind entails is of interest. Biko proposes that the decolonization of the mind is the black person who overcomes the inferiority complex bestowed upon them by colonization, opening the possibilities of rediscovering identity and creating a genuinely African culture.[234] Furthermore, there should be a recommitment to valuing human relationships and having "high regard for people, their property and for life in general; to reduce the hold of technology overall and to reduce the materialistic element that is slowly creeping into the African character."[235]

---

229. Wa Thiong'o, *Decolonising the Mind*, 17.

230. Wa Thiong'o, *Decolonising the Mind*, 108.

231. See Mofokeng, "Black Christology"; Mosala, "Black Theology"; Goba, "Toward a Quest"; Maimela, "Faith That Does Justice."

232. Biko, *Write What I Like*, 28.

233. Vellem, "Un-Thinking the West," 5.

234. Biko, *Write What I Like*, 70.

235. Biko, *Write What I Like*, 70–71.

Similarly, with a warning, Frantz Fanon proposes that the nationalistic consciousness of struggle should change into a social and political consciousness to safeguard "our countries from regression, paralysis, or collapse."[236] In other words, revolutionary leadership without the people's explicit appropriation of consciousness is without the necessary virtues of bringing about a society laden with a decolonized consciousness.

From a different perspective, a call for a decolonized consciousness is a call for a decolonized epistemology. In what I believe is a significant contribution to postcolonial thought in Southern Africa, Sabelo Ndlovu-Gatsheni, writes in his 2018 book, *Epistemic Freedom in Africa*, that "Epistemic freedom is fundamentally about the right to think, theorize, interpret the world, develop own methodologies and write from where one is located and unencumbered by Eurocentrism."[237] Thus, a decolonized mind is about, in an African context, "the African search for . . . self-rule, self-regeneration, self-understanding, self-definition, self-knowing and self-articulation of African issues after centuries of domination and silencing."[238]

Part and parcel of this decolonized epistemology is the need for a "decolonial attitude" within the academia.[239] The first aspect of a decolonial attitude is the "love of humanity" manifested in the credence that "all human beings were/are born into [a] valid and legitimate knowledge system." The second aspect is thus the ability to be concerned about epistemological dependence on Western epistemology. Thus, those concerned with decolonization are rational human beings who can see the crisis regarding epistemology and the more extensive system at work. After all, in the current market economy of capitalism, education "has become a very expensive commodity" laden with conflicts of affordability (#MustFall) and outsourcing. However, if Gayatri Spivak is to be taken seriously, "Western international economic interests" have always been part and parcel of Western epistemology.[240] The decolonization of epistemology will have to include a de-economization of education. A third aspect of the decolonial attitude is awareness and unmasking of what Berenstein calls "epistemic exploitation." Ndlovu-Gatsheni elaborates:

---

236. Fanon, *Wretched of the Earth*, 142–43.
237. Ndlovu-Gatsheni, *Epistemic Freedom in Africa*, 3.
238. Ndlovu-Gatsheni, *Epistemic Freedom in Africa*, 16.
239. Ndlovu-Gatsheni, *Epistemic Freedom in Africa*, 78.
240. Spivak, "Can the Subaltern Speak?," 271.

> In the face of decolonial struggles, the beneficiaries of the status quo degenerate into epistemic deafness and continuously ask the same questions over and over about what decolonization means.[241]

Therefore, epistemological decolonization as a decolonized attitude is embracing and developing analytic tools to deconstruct the epistemic exploitation of so-called normative methodologies.[242]

Terms of Violence

Before turning to the next section of this study, I want to contemplate for a moment the terms of violence Frantz Fanon adds to his understanding of the decolonization of the mind.

> In its bare reality, decolonization reeks of red-hot cannonballs and bloody knives. For the last can be the first only after a murderous and decisive confrontation between the two protagonists. This determination to have the last move up to the front, to have them clamber up (too quickly, say some) the famous echelons of an organized society, can only succeed by resorting to every means, including, of course, violence. —FRANTZ FANON[243]

I am convinced that Frantz Fanon's understanding of decolonization, as espoused in *The Wretched of the Earth*, both in the physical and mental universe, is impossible without violence. In the above quote, he seems to propose violence as the final act of decolonization. In another place, he states clearly that work towards decolonization is "to work towards the death of the colonist."[244] Once more, violence for Fanon is the means and terms through which the "colonized man liberates himself." Again, Fanon claims that the work of those who have been colonized is to "imagine every possible method of annihilating the colonist."[245]

---

241. Ndlovu-Gatsheni, *Epistemic Freedom in Africa*, 79.

242. In Tinyiko Maluleke's contemplation on Black and African Theologies in democratic South Africa, he suggests, in similar fashion, that alternative epistemological foundations for theology should be laid in South Africa. He believes that theology should take note of the alternative economic and social structures which are practised within Africa and follow suit in a theological manner. Maluleke, "Black and African Theologies," 16–18.

243. Fanon, *Wretched of the Earth*, 3.

244. Fanon, *Wretched of the Earth*, 44.

245. Fanon, *Wretched of the Earth*, 50.

The implication of Fanon's radical violence, which I have not found in other literature on postcolonial thought, poses a couple of problems. If he is correct in proposing that decolonization cannot occur without such radical violence, can decolonization ever take place? If we take seriously the idea that both the colonized and colonizer require decolonization in total,[246] does that mean the colonizer can only be decolonized when killed? Furthermore, does the violence promoted by Fanon not bring forth a similar brutalization of the colonized as violence brutalized the colonizer? Moreover, and I do not want to claim that violence is inherently immoral, how should homiletics go about contemplating this radical call to violence of Fanon?

Or maybe Fanon helps with the *terms* of postcolonial homiletics; postcolonial homiletics is a call to violent preaching and biblical hermeneutics.[247] Furthermore, a call to violent preaching and hermeneutics is a call to the truth about contextual realities. However, I will return to these ideas in the chapter on homiletics.

Moving the Centre

> In the sixteenth century, the emerging hegemonic imaginary of modernity was built around the figures of orbis and, more specifically, orbis universalis christianus. —WALTER MIGNOLO[248]

> The Eurocentric basis of seeing the world has often meant marginalizing into the periphery that which comes from the rest of the world. One historical particularity is generalized into a timeless and spaceless universality. —NGŨGĨ WA THIONG'O[249]

As is evident in the thoughts of Mignolo and Wa Thiong'o, colonization proposed the center of the world, of epistemology, of civilization, and of perspective to be Eurocentric, Christian (a Western interpretation of Christianity), and in its nature universal to all people. Thus, to think legitimately within the (neo)colonial framework is to center yourself in the perspective of the West. From the location of culture of those who are white, male, and of European descent, this comes most naturally. As Cornell and Seely show,

---

246. Césaire, *Discourse on Colonialism*, 41.

247. See Wepener and Pieterse, "Angry Preaching"; Wepener, *Kookpunt! Nadenke oor woede*.

248. Mignolo, "Many Faces of Cosmo-Polis," 726.

249. Wa Thiong'o, *Moving the Centre*, 43.

the irrational myth of modernity is built on the concept of "Man" as rational self—thus, maleness, Europeanness, and whiteness.[250] Ngũgĩ wa Thiong'o showcases that Joseph Conrad (the Polish-British writer) "wrote from the center of the empire."[251] Stephen Ellis suggests that the West became the universal center because of the type of control they exerted through the particular way colonization played out, with a specific vision of development.[252] In other words, Europe believed its institution and systems were the most advanced while transmitting that belief to the indigenous peoples.

Writing from this center brought forth (and still brings forth) misrepresentation of the other. An instance of misrepresentation takes place in Daniel Defoe's *Robinson Crusoe*. Herein, from the perspective of Defoe, Crusoe (the Western hero) confers humanity unto Friday (the non-Western stranger Crusoe meets) by teaching Friday the English language.[253] However, Friday was not without humanity nor a language before Crusoe arrived; it is only from the perspective of the empire that such a misrepresentation is both possible and acceptable. Never can Friday learn the language of revolt against the imagination of Crusoe's colonization.[254] Friday is thus representative of the colonized as portrayed by the perspective of the colonizer's center. In this way of thinking, the colonized can only become legitimately human when they privilege the colonizer's center.

As Ngũgĩ wa Thiong'o states, the colonized are "made to look to a distant neon light on a faraway hill flashing out the word EUROPE. Henceforth Europe and its languages would be the center of the universe."[255] When I was first confronted with the unveiling of the irrational myth that the West is the center of the universe, it seemed to be such an obvious error in perspective. However, that is the point; the irrational myth is of such power to colonize the mind that taking a perspective that is simultaneously not your own and actively working towards harming you has been normalized. It has been proposed as the only legitimate perspective for making sense of the world. Ngũgĩ wa Thiong'o is convinced that the problem of colonization arises not when a center's vision is proposed (even a Western

---

250. Cornell and Seely, *Spirit of Revolution*, 123.
251. Wa Thiong'o, *Moving the Centre*, 24.
252. Ellis, "South Africa," 9.
253. Wa Thiong'o, *Moving the Centre*, 33.
254. Wa Thiong'o, *Moving the Centre*, 34.
255. Wa Thiong'o, *Moving the Centre*, 50.

center) but rather when "people tried to use the vision from any one center and generalize it as the universal reality."[256]

After having unveiled the center. And understanding that Western civilization is promoted as the center of the universe with such violence that no other perspective is permitted, postcolonial thought moves the center.

> But it did point out the possibility of moving the center from its location in Europe towards a pluralism of centers; themselves being equally legitimate locations of the human imagination. —Ngũgĩ wa Thiong'o[257]

> Let's assume then that globalization is a set of designs to manage the world while cosmopolitanism is a set of projects toward planetary conviviality. —Walter Mignolo[258]

From the above quotes, it immediately strikes me that moving the center is not to dislocate the Western center and to replace it with a specific alternative center. What is proposed is instead "a plurality of centers"[259] or "a critical cosmopolitanism,"[260] which opens the way to a myriad of legitimate and life-giving locations for imagining the world. My expectation for a movement of the center was towards a new center which would have been the new norm. However, and I concede that my perspective presupposes the need for a normative understanding of life, a movement to a new legitimate center would have been a new form of colonization under a different name.

Returning to the plurality of centers, Ngũgĩ wa Thiong'o does not propose these centers to be exclusive.[261] On the contrary, he is quite keen on a borrowing and mutual give-and-take from one center to another. Even more, whether it be language or knowledge, Ngũgĩ wa Thiong'o is convinced that embracing "mutual fertilization" is beneficial to unleash a more significant potential for human imagination.[262] With a plurality of centers and the idea that the centers do not need to be, but instead, must

---

256. Wa Thiong'o, *Moving the Centre*, 22.
257. Wa Thiong'o, *Moving the Centre*, 26.
258. Mignolo, "Many Faces of Cosmo-Polis," 721.
259. Wa Thiong'o, *Moving the Centre*, 26.
260. Mignolo, "Many Faces of Cosmo-Polis," 723.
261. Wa Thiong'o, *Moving the Centre*, 40.
262. Wa Thiong'o, *Moving the Centre*, 40, 47.

not be exclusive from each other, I ask again, wherein lies the movement of the center?

As Ngũgĩ wa Thiong'o shows, moving the center lies in "absorbing the world," about being in the world, thinking about the world, perceiving reality, and thus about epistemological perspective.[263] After all, is it not more legitimate to view the world from one's location of culture as the center? And from here, ask how one center (and one's center) relates to other centers. Thus, the "question was not that of mutual exclusion between Africa and Europe but the basis and the starting point of their interaction."[264]

What Ngũgĩ wa Thiong'o is, in effect, speaking about is the "process of cognition."[265] He claims it begins not with universal principles but rather with looking at the particular contextual realities and forming from the specific that which is universal. However, this can never be considered universal, and the process of cognition must occur repeatedly in every center and as every center changes. At the same time, through this process, the newly found universal should be tested in the particular to see whether it can hold its own. Ngũgĩ wa Thiong'o thus calls for a "recovery of the philosophy of practice."[266] In practical theological terms, he calls for the recovery of the theology of practice, a theology of the context, people, and the particular center.

It interests me how Ngũgĩ wa Thiong'o's proposal might be read next to Richard Osmer's methodology for doing practical theology. As is well known in South African practical theological circles, Osmer asks four questions: "What is going on?" "Why is it going on?" "What ought to be going on?" and "How might we respond?"[267] His methodology begins with the particular. However, normativity flows from universal to specificity in the third question. The presupposition is that the Bible (or rather a Reformed interpretation of the Bible) is normative for practical theology. And from this universal normativity, a practical solution will be found for the particular context. However, if the legitimate center is moved towards many centers, depending on one's location of culture, this methodology is impossible. Mignolo concurs, stating that a macronarrative is problematic and the "crucial point is . . . why and from where [the beginning is

263. Wa Thiong'o, *Moving the Centre*, 27.
264. Wa Thiong'o, *Moving the Centre*, 27.
265. Wa Thiong'o, *Moving the Centre*, 44.
266. Wa Thiong'o, *Moving the Centre*, 44.
267. Osmer, *Practical Theology*, 4.

located]."²⁶⁸ Stated differently, and once more, any interpretation of the Bible (and Christianity), which proposes a normative narrative wherein life must fit or be made to fit, is problematic. Questions must, therefore, be asked of any interpretation of the Bible. Why is this the interpretation of a text? Who stands to benefit, and who is excluded? From where (which perspective) is this text interpreted? How does the center, from where this text is interpreted, relate to other centers?

At the same time, it would be shortsighted to propose that all theologians (and homileticians in particular) are aware of their positionality within coloniality and uncritical about such a positionality. Concerning the first, I've already touched on the importance of stating one's position.[269] Regarding the latter, many scholars within the colonial perspective have been critical of the state of theology during their times (Isaiah, Jeremiah, Jesus, Karl Barth, Allan Boesak, Johan Cilliers, Walter Brueggemann, to name but a few). I would go as far as to claim that responsible theology searches for new avenues of thinking. However, as Mignolo reasons, a postcolonial understanding of homiletics will have to consider the possibility that criticism of coloniality from within the framework of coloniality does not move the epistemological center.[270] In other words, criticism of Reformed Christianity through historical Reformed sources and epistemology cannot bring forth a plurality of centers. Instead, from such a position, the center stays the same. Even more, and I think this is a feature of BTL, proposing another hermeneutic center (for BTL, the experience of the black oppressed) is merely universalizing another center. By so doing, BTL commits the same epistemological wrongdoing of a Christianity, which proposes Europe and European culture as the center of Christianity.

One could even criticize postcolonial study's entire endeavor of moving the center beyond colonialism and yet, at the same time, being stuck with the language and ideas of colonialism. As Simone Drichel so eloquently states:

> It seems that postcolonialism is informed by contradictory impulses: it needs both to move "post-*the other*" to be properly *post*-colonial and yet at the same time to maintain the other as its

---

268. Mignolo, "Many Faces of Cosmo-Polis," 722.
269. See Vellem, "Un-Thinking the West."
270. Mignolo, "Many Faces of Cosmo-Polis," 723.

foundational or, perhaps more appropriately, undeconstructable concern.[271]

In other words, and I think this is important, as much as postcolonial thought calls for a movement of the center, a call to be off-center, the question is not only whereto but also in which manner. Once again, it is not only the content that is essential for this endeavor of forging postcolonial thought for preaching but also the terms.[272] Returning to Drichel, if *the other* is an essential concern for postcolonial thought, yet *the other* is only other because of a centralized Western perspective, how would postcolonial thought reconfigure *the other* to incorporate a plurality of centers adequately?

A Decentered, Fragmented Identity

The third focal image I have delimited from postcolonial thought for this study is a decentered, fragmented identity. As I have alluded to, postcolonial thought has considered *the other* as an essential concern. However, *the other*—as a concept—supposes a colonial perspective, a view *toward* those who are deemed illegitimate. In other words, *the other* is an identity perceived from a Western center. Thus, the same question again: how would postcolonial thought reconfigure *the other* to adequately incorporate at least an alternative center as a location of perspective?

In postcolonial thought, I believe many images are essential for understanding a decentered and fragmented identity: agency, hybridity, border identity, mimicry, creativity, and improvisation. All these images are intertwined and interrelated in a bodily manner for a decentered, fragmented identity. Not just in perceiving (the other's) bodies, but firstly in having bodies. However, I want to contemplate a decentered, fragmented identity in four movements: 1) the relationship between a decentered, fragmented identity and time; 2) the concept of hybridity; 3) the body of a decentered, fragmented identity; and 4) a critical evaluation of academia and a decentered, fragmented identity.

---

271. Drichel, "Time of Hybridity," 588.
272. Mignolo, "Delinking," 459.

Comparison between (BTL) & Postcolonial Thought

Identity and Time

> Only a non-exposure to time—as that which brings about change—can produce a representation that is "arrested" and "fixated."
> —Simone Drichel[273]

> And, paradoxically, it is only through a structure of splitting and displacement . . . that the architecture of the new historical subject emerges at the limits of representation itself. —Homi Bhabha[274]

From the Western center of coloniality, the person who is not like the normative "Man" is perceived as an object of brutality, unsophistication, and backwardness.[275] In the best cases, this other person is a subject with a unique history and perspective, but still *the other*. In the worst cases, this other person has no history, culture, or human value. Thus, viewed from a colonial center, she is not as one should be. She is, therefore, devoid of existence except through the stereotypes laid upon her by the Western gaze. She is what the Western center perceives her to be, and she will always be such. Alternatively, as Drichel suggests, the Western gaze upon the other without exposure to time brings forth a representation or stereotype which is arrested and fixed.[276]

Ngũgĩ wa Thiong'o shows that the Western perspective is, in its very being, a racist perspective. It depicts Africans as good once they have accepted and incorporated the Western perspective for themselves or evil when they refuse the colonial perspective.[277] Once more, the other is conceived as human (yet a second-class citizen) when siding with the colonial powers or savage when standing against colonization.

There is, however, another layer of representation from a colonial perspective. Vuyani Vellem is deeply critical of the Western epistemological thought often present in BTL.[278] A case in point is the insistence that God stands on the side of the poor, the marginalized, and the oppressed.[279] Here we find a depiction of a-temporal stereotypes even though BTL wants to

---

273. Drichel, "Time of Hybridity," 589.
274. Bhabha, *Location of Culture*, 217.
275. Cornell and Seely, *Spirit of Revolution*, 123.
276. Drichel, "Time of Hybridity," 589.
277. Wa Thiong'o, *Moving the Centre*, 34.
278. Vellem, "Un-Thinking the West," 1.
279. See Mofokeng, "Cross in the Search," 48; Boesak, "'Hope Unprepared to Accept Things.'"

make the point that these people represent the place where God stands. However, concepts such as poor, marginalized, and oppressed presuppose a fixed identity that can neither be changed (or at least not changed by the labor of those deemed poor, marginalized, and oppressed) nor reinterpreted. Once more, even as BTL tries to move beyond the stereotypes of colonialism, it uses the same stereotypes to make its point. And therein, the point becomes lost because the gaze is still a Western gaze, a gaze from a colonial power, an a-temporal representation.

Homi Bhabha proposes that the postcolonial world, delinking from Western historical myths, perceptions, and the emerging awareness of cultural diversity, has brought forth new possibilities of being in the world. He proposes that "the new historical subject emerges at the limits of representation itself."[280] Stated differently, only once the Western representation of the other reaches its limit within the existence of a decolonized consciousness can the new historical subject emerge. Here, I propose Homi Bhabha's "decentered, fragmented subject" as an adequate first movement into a new representation of the postcolonial identity.[281]

Once more, I reiterate the importance of time for postcolonial identity. A decentered and fragmented identity is a timeous, ever-changing, dynamic, never an a-temporally represented stereotype. A decentered and fragmented identity may move beyond ideas of decentering and fragmentation towards a centered and structured identity. Nevertheless, even a movement towards a new identity underscores that the postcolonial identity is timeous and not constructed to any one representation. Even more, after having constructed and presented the postcolonial identity, such a representation is already dated.

Hybridity

> In other words, we do not need to move "post-*the other*" only because this other—as hybrid other—stands in relation to temporality. —SIMONE DRICHEL[282]

Simone Drichel proposes that culture as a concept of delimiting any individual or group is a colonial endeavor of "othering," holding one captive to

---

280. Bhabha, *Location of Culture*, 217.
281. Bhabha, *Location of Culture*, 216.
282. Drichel, "Time of Hybridity," 589.

the terms of a culture with its traditions and customs of the past. She goes on to show that the delimiting of culture presupposes that the only truly universal human nature is that of the European. She makes a point that the label of culture (and race and ethnicity) placed on any subject produces colonial categories to withhold certain people from "an assumed universal human nature."[283] She proposes a hybrid identity for the postcolonial subject in counteracting the stereotyping of the colonial perspective.

However, to ensure that hybridity does not become the new fixed center for thinking, Drichel speaks of a hybrid identity as "*c/entre.*"[284] Take note of the slash, which Drichel understands as "a silent reminder . . . that this centre is decentred, both split and double."[285] Drichel takes cognizance of Derrida's description of ever-changing fixed centers, thereby heeding the warning of making hybridity the new fixed center. BTL has precisely done this with the privileged position of the marginalized, poor, and excluded. The positionality of the marginalized became the proposed new fixed position of doing theology, and all other centers, mainly European, Western, and white theological centers, were abdicated as illegitimate. On the one hand, there is truth in the critique of white theological centers, but the critique should have been focused on the fact that, to a large extent, white theology proposes one center as normative. Put another way, when the position of the Black theological center as the hermeneutical privileging of the black experience became *the sine qua non* for interpreting the Bible and doing theology, the proposal was merely to shift the center to a new fixed position.

Returning to the hybrid identity, what is meant by a hybrid identity? What would such an identity entail? Where is hybridity to be found? And what does hybridity bring to the table for a decentered, fragmented identity?

In Homi Bhabha's contemplation on hybridity, he proposes, following Fanon, that the formation of a hybrid identity becomes possible during a disruption in the spatial realities of fixedness. This implies that during, for instance, the struggle for liberation, a newness in space emerges, a discontinuity in time, bringing forth the possibility (rather certainty) of negotiation and translation.[286] The implication is a third space, no longer the colonial space, and not yet that which is envisioned as the goal of liberation, but a

---

283. Drichel, "Time of Hybridity," 589.
284. Drichel, "Time of Hybridity," 605.
285. Drichel, "Time of Hybridity," 605.
286. Bhabha, *Location of Culture*, 38.

third space of possibilities. Herein, the identity of the people has formed anew. Even more, the cultural preconceptions and stereotypes are dislodged from their a-temporality, and the people are "free to negotiate and translate their cultural identities" for themselves.[287]

However, the possibility of forming new identities does not automatically lead to hybridity. As a case in point, in the South African context, Desmond Tutu called for a hybrid identity in 1994, the so-called "Rainbow Nation." What played out was the emergence of some hybrid identities and communities. However, by 2020 it seems that racial and cultural disparities are once more the order of the day, most alarmingly amongst the so-called "born frees" (those born after 1994).

Nevertheless, Bhabha is optimistic about the possibility of an emergence of "an *inter*national culture," a culture that incorporates both what has been inherited from colonization by the indigenous culture(s) and what has anew come to the fore through the process of negotiation in the third space.[288] Furthermore, this hybridity must not be limited by a temporal presentation of identity but is open to becoming "the other of ourselves."[289]

Emmanuel Lartey's contemplation of a public ritual in Elmina, Ghana sheds light on what hybridity may entail in a liturgical context. A first insight was the ecumenical nature of the liturgy. Adherents of three faith traditions partook in the liturgy—Christians, Muslims, and adherents of traditional African religion.[290] A second important aspect was the inclusion of libation in the liturgy.[291] Although Christian missionary endeavors have been significantly antagonistic to libation, within this liturgical space, it was not only tolerated but justified as essentially honoring one's father and mother as ordered through the law of Moses. Thirdly, the liturgy's political implications brought forth a new formation of identity.

On the one hand, a recognition of culpability by the rulers, albeit culpability of their ancestors. This recognition brings forth an identity of self-critique, which I believe fits better with a hybrid identity than that of a fixed and normative center. On the other hand, the liturgy involved cleansing the culpable and the victims (or their offspring).[292] Lartey is convinced that this

---

287. Bhabha, *Location of Culture*, 38.
288. Bhabha, *Location of Culture*, 38.
289. Bhabha, *Location of Culture*, 39.
290. Lartey, *Postcolonializing God*, 59.
291. Lartey, *Postcolonializing God*, 60.
292. Lartey, *Postcolonializing God*, 60–61.

cleansing is the only way to transcend the stereotypes of the past "for both time and space to be transfigured."

The Body and the Decentered, Fragmented Identity

> Indeed, any formulation of theological anthropology that takes body and body marks seriously risks absolutizing or fetishizing what can be seen (race and sex), constructed (gender), represented (sexuality), expressed (culture), and regulated (social order). . . . But what makes such risk imperative is the location and condition of bodies in empire; what makes such risk obligatory is that the body of Jesus of Nazareth, the Word made flesh, was subjugated in empire. —MARY COPELAND[293]

I take the queue from Mary Copeland to contemplate the body as an essential aspect of a decentered, fragmented identity for a postcolonial point of departure. She makes the point that it is a biblical imperative to contemplate the body about its relationship with empire. Her reasoning is linked to the identity of Jesus of Nazareth; his body was subjugated to empire. Thus, theological contemplation is imperative. However, from a postcolonial perspective, the imperative of contemplating the body can be done without any theological forerunner. The contemplation of the body for a decentered, fragmented identity within postcolonial thought flows quite seamlessly from the reality of colonization within modernity. That the body is of importance is without a doubt. No one exists without the existence of a body, and the power and injustices of the irrational myth are centered on a European gaze of the body of the other. This is always in the light that the West is the center of thought, and all other locations of cultures must be integrated into the Western center.

However, with the breakage of the irrational myth of modernity, the body of this new identity becomes of great importance. Emmanuel Lartey proposes three actions associated with the postcolonial identity: mimicry, improvisation, and creativity.[294]

Regarding mimicry, the postcolonial subject mimics the actions of the colonizer. With mimicry, there is a double goal: firstly, to showcase that the abilities of the colonizer are not beyond the abilities of the other. Stated differently, the activities of the colonizer can be mimicked rightly. The second

---

293. Copeland, *Enfleshing Freedom*, 56–57.
294. Lartey, *Postcolonializing God*, 126–28.

goal is to mock the colonizer. Herein mimicry plays the colonizer to be a fool. It repeats the activity of the colonizer but with a humorous twist. However, I believe a third aspect is essential for the insights already revealed in this book: mimicry as assimilation, inclusion, and borrowing of knowledge from other centers.[295] In this instance, mimicry serves to be inclusive and positive concerning alternative centers. The decolonized consciousness has been reached here, and equality is presupposed amongst centers.

The second action is that of improvisation. According to Lartey, improvisation is making do with what is available.[296] I think the point is quite clear, from a location of identity that is decentered and fragmented, that the normative methods of existing in this world do not apply. A hybrid identity cannot but have to improvise within a world still constructed by a Western gaze. This, I reckon, is especially true about a globalized capitalist world. As Thomas Piketty shows, wealth inequality has been brought on by increased capital/income ratio disparity.[297] In other terms, activity in the form of labor cannot create wealth in the same manner and to the same degree as capital. The postcolonial person must work within these confines. However, both in the daily struggle of existence and the political implication of daily existence, improvisation acts as a manner of subverting the status quo of the current system. Moreover, a new way of thinking, politics, and economies can be born out of the improvisation of the postcolonial person.

As a case in point, we may look at the African American jazz singer Cab Calloway who performed in Harlem, New York, during the 1930s. Nate Sloan states that Calloway was able to mimic white singing and improvise a new type of singer, which came to be known as the "Harlem voice."[298] Interesting is the fluidity of Calloway's identity. As Sloan claims, "Calloway resisted a uniform identity," wherein he incorporated various vocal approaches.[299] Interestingly enough, Calloway was not considered black enough as he had a lighter skin color, adding to the fluidity of his identity and bringing forth a decentered identity as others questioned his exact racial location.[300]

    295. Wa Thiong'o, *Moving the Centre*, 40.
    296. Lartey, *Postcolonializing God*, 127.
    297. Piketty, *Capital in the Twenty-First Century*, 336.
    298. Sloan, "Constructing Cab Calloway," 392.
    299. Sloan, "Constructing Cab Calloway," 393.
    300. Sloan, "Constructing Cab Calloway," 394.

The third action of the postcolonial person is that of creativity. Emmanuel Lartey is convinced that creativity showcases the epitome of the postcolonial person's agency.[301] Through creativity, the postcolonial person emerges as a free being, confident and void of anxiety about the Western gaze. The creativity of the postcolonial subject sprouts forth the moment of realization that she is fully human and equal to all people. Furthermore, it is in creativity that the postcolonial person realizes that she has indeed been made in the image of God; for as God is creative in the act of creation, so too, the postcolonial person is *imago Dei* in the act of her creativity.

The Academia

> "Indeed, the concrete experience that is the guarantor of the political appeal of prisoners, soldiers, and schoolchildren is disclosed through the concrete experience of the intellectual, the one who diagnoses the episteme."—GAYATRI SPIVAK[302]

> "Furthermore, the danger is always that the agency discourse becomes removed from the real contexts where people are expected or seen to be agents. If the agency discourse remains only and mainly a 'Whites only and males only' discourse, with Blacks and women merely supplying the raw material and the case studies and the anecdotes, the danger of constructing a fantastic, artificial, and romanticized agent is there."—TINYIKO MALULEKE AND SAROJINI NADAR[303]

Taking the cue from Spivak, Maluleke, and Nadar, the postcolonial person's representation within the academia should be negotiated continuously. However, can academia represent the postcolonial person? How do we represent the postcolonial person?

Moreover, especially in the context of South African homiletics, which has been overwhelmed with Reformed homiletics scholars, how do we think about preaching and the agency of the postcolonial person? How do I place something on the table without misrepresenting the postcolonial person? Stated differently, am I merely representing the postcolonial subject in my own image?

---

301. Lartey, *Postcolonializing God*, 128.

302. Spivak, "Can the Subaltern Speak?," 275.

303. Maluleke and Nadar, "Alien Fraudsters," 7.

To return to Spivak, Maluleke, and Nadar: their opinion regarding the representation of other persons by the academia, and more specifically by the white academia, is harmful. I do not think there is a solution for whether such representation is viable. Instead, I think the paradox must remain. Yes, on the one hand, the representation of the postcolonial person within academia is problematic. On the other hand, academia should be an open and experimental place to move beyond normative representations, even if representations of the postcolonial person may be problematic. The point should be that with the failures and mistakes of representation, new avenues should be sought to move towards a more accurate representation of the postcolonial subject.

CONCLUSION

At the onset of this chapter, I asked two questions: How do BTL and postcolonial thought relate to one another? What would it mean to consider postcolonial scholars seriously?

Through my genealogical tracing (albeit reductionistic) of both BTL and postcolonial thought, I propose the following three markers to delimit the relationship between BTL and postcolonial theory: 1) BTL is an authentic theological endeavor in postcolonializing; 2) however, BTL falls short in its attempt at postcolonializing, both in its epistemology and in its promotion of a new normative center of perspective; 3) postcolonial thought opens some exciting avenues of theologizing for BTL and my endeavor within homiletics.

BTL's insistence on working from a different center than Western theology, I am convinced, showcases a postcolonial movement. In the change of perspective to the lived experience of black people during apartheid, BTL could innovatively and creatively transcend the hermeneutics of Western theology—both with regard to contextual realities and biblical interpretation. At the same time, this change of perspective or center brought forth new imaginations of the future, how the world could be constructed, and how politics and the economy could be more just.

Since democracy in South Africa, BTL has become more ecumenical in its self-understanding, another postcolonial endeavor. It has become more inclusive of the African heritage as espoused by African theology and AICs. There is an apparent move away from normative theological understanding, towards the lived experience of Africans, including their position not as victims but as active agents in the world.

However, Black Theology of Liberation dangles very closely to a position still confined to the epistemology of Western thinking.

This is especially the case regarding proposing the black experience (specifically the black experience as a marginal, poor, and excluded location of culture) as the new normative position. As shown in this chapter, the representation of identity as a fixed identity presupposes a Western way of stereotyping. Put another way, in an endeavor to promote the position of the black experience of oppression, the epistemological confines of Western thought have captivated BTL to such an extent that BTL has not yet defined adequate methods to move beyond Western limits. Yet, during democracy, there have been strides in locating the black experience outside of oppression, such as in the agency of black people.

From a different perspective, the late Vuyani Vellem made enormous strides in dislocating Western epistemology for BTL through the insights of postcolonial thought. Yet, I am unconvinced that Vellem's enterprise has taken root in BTL's larger South African movements. Hopefully, Vellem's legacy will produce excellent black theologians capable of taking BTL seriously, critiquing its shortcomings, and moving beyond to new avenues of thought for human well-being and liberation.

The postcolonial ideas I have delimited in this chapter open some exciting avenues both for Black Theology of Liberation to consider and for South African homiletics.

I have delimited three main themes in postcolonial thought. These are unveiling the irrational myth, decolonizing the mind, and moving the center and postcolonial identity. These themes, I have suggested, produce a new way of thinking, not only in content but also in form. Within the following chapters, I will endeavor to find ways to integrate these three themes within the studies of homiletics, liturgy, and hermeneutics. After all, a contemplation of preaching is lacking, in my opinion, if it does not consider the whole spectrum of the worship service within the lived experience of the congregation.

CHAPTER 2

Postcolonial Preaching? Contemplation on Postcolonial Thought and Homiletics

THE CURRENT SOUTH AFRICAN situation is one where issues of decolonization are ever-present. Decolonization is under discussion in formal settings such as parliament regarding policies on land expropriation[1] and theological education at the university about visions of decolonial syllabi.[2] Decolonization is further under discussion in informal settings: insourcing protests at tertiary institutions, ritual offerings in the backyards of the rich,[3] and the #FeesMustFall movements.[4]

At the same time, South Africans are very religious, with 85.6 percent having indicated in the 2013 General Household Survey that they are Christians.[5] Moreover, 5 percent affiliate with African Traditional Religion (ATR), 2 percent with Islam, and 1 percent with Hinduism. Overall, 93.6 percent of South Africans affiliated themselves with a religious tradition. Thus, in the same context of underlying decolonial discourse, thousands of sermons are preached and heard weekly. Preaching is indeed a practice that plays a significant role in the lives of South Africans. As a homiletic endeavor within the South African context, I must ask this: What would a form of preaching entail which seriously considers postcolonial thought?

1. Makinana, "Parliament Gives Go-Ahead."

2. Kaunda, "Denial of African Agency," 75–92; Naidoo, "Overcoming Alienation," 1–9; Venter, *Theology and the (Post)Apartheid Condition*; Wepener et al., "Tradition of Practical Theology," 146–51.

3. Maphanga, "Protest to 'Reclaim' Clifton Beach."

4. Chirume, "Nelson Mandela University Protest Ends."

5. Statistics South Africa, *General Household Survey*, 12.

Postcolonial Preaching?

To answer this question, I will contemplate three movements for this chapter: One, delimiting markers for postcolonial homiletics. Two, a proposal for a preliminary definition of postcolonial preaching using the insights gathered in chapter 1 of this book. And three, a sermon as an attempt at postcolonial preaching.

DELIMITING MARKERS FOR HOMILETICS

Faith

> Inasmuch as it *is* anything, preaching is a radical, foolish act of faith—and I particularly appreciate Richard Kearney's conception of faith as "knowing you don't know anything absolutely about absolutes." —Jacob Myers[6]

In my understanding of postcolonial thought, there is no reason to propose that preaching must occur. Moreover, the proposal that preaching is imperative "in the service of God to strengthen the church"[7] cannot hold water for postcolonial homiletics. After all, too many presuppositions exist within such imperatives. Firstly, there is a normative imperative for living in the world: *in service of God*. Secondly, the existence of a community known as the church and its continued existence. Thirdly, preaching has the ipso facto goal of strengthening the church, whatever that may imply.

Thus, my first question in contemplating postcolonial homiletics is this: why preach? And why preaching? Stated otherwise, there is no apparent reason for the act of preaching. When considering the postcolonial endeavor of moving the center, there is no reason to take preaching as an undisputed absolute. From the postcolonial perspective, as I have delimited in the previous chapter, the church, the ministry, the Bible, and even faith are all disputable. However, from the contextual analysis of the South African situation, especially regarding the Christian religion, faith is a reality. In my reading of postcolonial thought, the context must be taken seriously, not only in the sheer number (quantity) of religious people but also in the influence religion and preaching have on people's lives (quality).

Furthermore, as per Jacob Myers, preaching's existence does not necessarily flow from a normative position; it flows merely from the view

---

6. Myers, *Preaching Must Die!*, 8.
7. Wilson, "General Editor's Preface," xxv.

that people have faith and the need to act on their faith through preaching and worship.[8] In his understanding, preaching is not centered on truth, certainty, and absolutes but rather on uncertainty, fluidity, and foolishness through the faith people possess. Thus, why preach? Because faith is an essential aspect of the South African context.

However, why preaching? Why not religious speech? Why do I contemplate preaching? Stated otherwise, as I have shown in chapter 1, the center of thinking molds the perspective from which theologizing takes place. For postcolonial homiletics, the center of thinking must be moved, and contemplation cannot sprout from certainty or a fixed center, far less a Western center as normative. However, at the same time, my choice to seriously consider preaching as an act of faith within the Christian community sprouts from my belief that preaching is essential. Thus, I choose to center preaching as the focus of this book and as an essential practice in the Christian community alongside other Christian practices.

However, is it possible to center preaching without centering Western theological thought? Johan Cilliers' contemplation of why preaching is essential concludes that preaching is vital, for it is words entrusted to preachers that must be spoken.[9] Although he does not indicate who has entrusted these words, I believe his understanding is that God has entrusted these words to be preached. From a postcolonial perspective, I cannot take the same concrete stance regarding what God has supposedly given to be said and that preaching must, therefore, take place.

Language

However, as I have shown in the previous chapter, Black theologians and postcolonial thinkers may help as interlocutors for a postcolonial raison d'être for preaching.

In this line of thinking, preaching could be understood not as an imperative given by a greater authority but as an imaginative and inspiring language of struggle. Thus, preaching's existence sprouts not from the imperative that preaching must exist but rather from the location of culture where struggle is the reality of everyday life.

From a postcolonial perspective, preaching is the supreme linguistic act of struggle within the religious community:

8. Myers, *Preaching Must Die!*, 8.
9. Cilliers, *Living Voice of the Gospel*, 20–21.

Postcolonial Preaching?

> The call for the rediscovery and the resumption of our language is a call for a regenerative reconnection with the millions of revolutionary tongues in Africa and the world over demanding liberation. It is a call for the rediscovery of the real language of humankind: the language of struggle. It is the universal language underlying all speech and words of our history. Struggle. Struggle makes history. Struggle makes us. In struggle is our history, our language and our being.[10]

> I am suggesting that preaching Jesus Christ means preaching liberation and transformation. . . . This kind of preaching deals with poverty, fairness, justice, humility, and other social, economic, and moral problems that face the church and society.[11]

Two markers are of importance in this line of thinking. Firstly, struggle is born out of a particular location of culture. It is not from a position of comfort and power but from powerlessness and discomfort.[12] Thus, for preaching to be a language of struggle, the irrational myth of the modern utopia and a fixed identity must be resisted.

In other words, postcolonial preaching is a truly human endeavor where we are honest with the reality of our existence. We are not the fixed and stereotyped "Man" of modernity, existing on the myth of a capability of all things.[13] But we have a postcolonial identity, struggling to form identity in contextual realities: "poverty, fairness, justice, humility, and other social, economic, and moral problems that face the church and society."[14]

During apartheid in South Africa, Allan Boesak proposed the existence of theology as "joining the struggle for human liberation in Africa."[15] Postcolonial preaching is aware of the necessity of struggle, yet not stuck in a contextuality long past, the struggle for a decolonization of the mind. As I have shown in chapter 1, this is an ideological struggle against mental control from any central authority or tyrant and the subsequent construction

---

10. Wa Thiong'o, *Decolonising the Mind*, 108.

11. Harris, *Preaching Liberation*, 37–38.

12. It is not clear to me that the ideals of empathy as allies in other people's struggle conceptualize the reality of the human experience. Under such circumstances, struggle belongs to only some people—those conceptualized as victims. Instead, given enough time, tragedy will befall us all, and it is under such circumstances and understanding of time, that struggle is universal.

13. Cornell and Seely, *Spirit of Revolution*, 123.

14. Harris, *Preaching Liberation*, 37–38.

15. Boesak, *Black and Reformed*, 81.

of other ways of existing in the world. In this consideration, the tyrant can and will change, and constructing new ways of existing in the world will not be a one-off antidote nor the construction of an ideology that can never be fully implemented, even though its adherents consistently lament that the lack of implementation—in perpetuity.

In Jürgen Moltmann's contemplation of the kingdom of heaven, he comments: "In history and in this life believers experience 'the servant form of God's kingdom' in the suffering Christ."[16] I propose that this servant form of God's kingdom, the experience of God's kingdom in the penultimate of our lives, can be considered the postcolonial struggle. In this form of struggle, the kingdom of heaven's existence is in the joy of our existence, along with the joy of God's existence. This joy sprouts into thanksgiving, praise, and the celebration of life.[17] In this, we find the most incredible joy—struggle as "dreaming to change the world."[18]

Rhetoric

I have so far only touched on the subject of language. However, preaching has to do with the content of language (what) and the terms of language (how). The question must then be asked, what would postcolonial rhetoric entail? I propose three focal images for postcolonial rhetoric: struggle, foolishness, and anger.

I have contemplated the content of a language of struggle. However, a language of struggle is also rhetorical; it has to do with the how of preaching. In my understanding of struggle as rhetoric, I propose that postcolonial preaching is constantly en route to the destination of a decolonized consciousness. This means that to preach postcolonially is to struggle to speak. At the same time, the irrational myths of colonization, as both authoritarian and revolutionary, are thoroughly developed within its rhetoric form and marketed through social media, academia, and ecclesial communities. The rhetoric of postcolonial preaching is an attempt at transcending irrational myths and imagining a different world.

Once more, the decentering nature of postcolonial preaching brings forth rhetoric which inherently is to struggle against the rhetoric powers which absolutize and centralize the ideology of irrational myths as

---

16. Moltmann, *Coming of God*, 323.
17. Moltmann, *Coming of God*, 323.
18. Wa Thiong'o, *Decolonising the Mind*, 108.

fundamental to existence. At the same time, any centralized ideology must be struggled against. This means the fundamentalism within faith communities is just as problematic in its rhetoric as the irrational myth. Furthermore, where fundamentalism believes that its missional effort (and rhetoric of such missional effort) can bring forth the kingdom of God,[19] postcolonial preaching knows that such bringing forth of God's kingdom is impossible. The breaking through of God's kingdom is only in fragments. To preach postcolonially is to accept that our lives and words are those of struggle.

Returning to the irrational myth of colonization, Walter Brueggemann makes the following claim: "Empowered and humbled by the mandate of scripture, the preacher must counter the rhetoric of popular patriotism and witness to God's sovereignty over nations."[20] Writing from the United States of America, Brueggemann focuses on how the irrational myth has revealed itself in that context, popular patriotism. Taking the queue from Brueggemann, postcolonial preaching should rhetorically counter the rhetoric of the irrational myth. Furthermore, the last part is essential, "witness to God's sovereignty over nations." This witness to the ultimate power of God and the reminder of the penultimate power of nations (under the spell of the irrational myths political entities wrongly believe that they are ultimate) has to be repeated time and again. To witness is to struggle. The world and the powers under the irrational myths do not listen and do not hear. The task of postcolonial preaching is to speak and speak again. And even if not heard, keep speaking, preaching, struggling.

Brueggemann proposes: "We may then move beyond analysis to alternative, and finally set our hearts and minds on the evangelical task of empowering the faithful to alternative forms of citizenship."[21] Yes, indeed, so too for postcolonial preaching. The decolonization of the mind is the goal towards which the postcolonial preacher moves. However, in speaking and preaching, postcolonial preaching is thoroughly aware of the struggle against the irrational myths towards decolonizing the mind. If anything, this movement from one to the other is merely an attempt, a process. The postcolonial preacher does, therefore, not work with the rhetoric of certainty but the rhetoric of uncertainty. She is attempting to say something that moves the mind and heart towards postcolonial thought—proposing

---

19. Stockwell, "Fundamentalisms and the Shalom of God," 268.
20. Brueggemann, "Patriotism for Citizens," 336.
21. Brueggemann, "Patriotism for Citizens," 336.

a different way of seeing the world. Words such as "I think," "maybe we should look at the text from this perspective," and "let us think together" are not outside the framework of postcolonial preaching as the rhetoric of struggle and struggling together to make sense of the world in conversation with the faithful within their context.

> The gospel is foolishness. Preaching is folly. Preachers are fools. The foolishness goes all the way down, encompassing finally the rhetoric of preaching. Preaching fools employ a rhetoric of folly. Like preaching fools themselves, this rhetoric interrupts the conventions and rationalities of the old age and creates a liminal space at the juncture of the ages; it seeks to reframe perspective and invites discernment of the inbreaking new creation.[22]

Closely related to the rhetoric of struggle, but with a different emphasis, is the rhetoric of foolishness proposed by Charles Campbell and Johan Cilliers. For Campbell and Cilliers, preaching as a rhetoric of foolishness revolves around the idea that preaching is unable to "control the gospel in rigid figures or forms."[23] Thus, preaching can never be a centralization of an agenda, an ideology, a privileged identity, or a centralized perspective. Thus, in my attempt to reframe Campbell and Cilliers' idea of foolish preaching, postcolonial preaching is the Holy Spirit decentralizing and fragmenting the preacher's rhetoric.

This folly of preaching is an interruption of irrational myths. Even within the Christian religion, irrational myths require expansion and propagated repetition. I am convinced that this expansion is proposed, on the one hand, through fundamentalism and the ensuing gospel of capitalist prosperity,[24] and on the other hand, through nationalism, be it Afrikaner nationalism[25] or African nationalism with the cry that the African National Congress (ANC) will reign until Jesus comes.[26] As well as the more recent revolutionary impetuses of so-called "woke" movements in academia.[27]

Campbell and Cilliers' rhetoric of folly proposes that the gospel is itself a decentered and fragmented, always in flow, reforming, reframing, and fragmented with regards to any attempt at rhetoric of absolutes.

22. Campbell and Cilliers, *Preaching Fools*, 181.
23. Campbell and Cilliers, *Preaching Fools*, 181.
24. See Stockwell, "Fundamentalisms and the Shalom of God."
25. See Cilliers, "Preaching between Assimilation and Separation."
26. See Ngoepe, "ANC Will Rule."
27. See Haidt, "Why the Past 10 Years."

Postcolonial Preaching?

Finally, a mode of angry preaching may as much be necessitated in the contextual realities of South Africa. In the previous chapter, I contemplated Frantz Fanon's insistence that decolonization cannot occur without violence. As postcolonial preaching has to do with the decolonization of the mind, and faith, I propose that the violence of Fanon should be espoused in the rhetoric of anger for postcolonial preaching. This is not a novum movement within South African theology or homiletics. Allan Boesak, Cas Wepener, and Hennie Pieterse have proposed that anger is necessary as part of the rhetoric of preaching contextually in South Africa:

> It is a righteous anger because of injustice done to others, the refusal to meekly accept what is wrong, because it is a wrong done to someone created in the image of God. It is anger against the arrogance of power, against the sinful cowardice of feigned neutrality while benefiting from the fruits of injustice and exploitation. It is anger that refuses to give in to hopelessness and resists what drives us to despair. It is the anger of injured but unbowed dignity.[28]

> South Africans are angry and the nation has indeed reached boiling point. . . . As a nation South Africans should not be cured of their anger, but should rather be assisted to embody and through embodiment express their anger in meaningful ways. Acts of aggressions should be condemned; by way of comparison an expression of anger can also be a sign of hope showing that people still care.[29]

The poor in South Africa have been promised the world and received very little. It is at the location of struggle where the most anger lies against this reality. Reading the scriptural text from the positionality of those whose lives have not gone according to their dreams and hopes showcases the deep frustration and should come to the fore through a rhetoric of anger.

Neither the preacher nor the congregation can tolerate preaching that ignores the contextual realities, claiming "peace, peace" when there is no peace. No longer can the preacher, nor the congregation, act as if the status quo, which implies the suppression of reality, is the will of God. No longer can the preacher preach as if the world is not burning, as if there is no struggle, as if our people are not under constant economic and political pressure for mere survival. No longer can the preacher claim that Jesus is only the Lord of our hearts.

---

28. Boesak, *Dare We Speak of Hope?*, 51.
29. Wepener and Pieterse, "Angry Preaching," 404–5.

Postcolonial Homiletics?

Angry preaching is a rhetorical call to realism and empathy to experience, name, and live within the reality of the South African condition. It is the expression of the lived experience of the postcolonial person in its most concrete terms. In anger, we are found to be most human and honest about the South African situation. In the words of Eusebius McKaiser: "I am angry. I am fucking angry. I am angry . . . [we] often pretend we [see the moral stains of the society we live in]—a charity run here, fake integration projects there, and so on—but the structures of our society remain monumentally unjust."[30]

Wepener and Pieterse propose two more route markers for angry preaching. One, angry preaching should be accompanied by angry listening.[31] In postcolonial terms, there should be an open, third space, where angry preaching is welcomed and not subdued or opposed. Two, angry preaching should stand alongside angry liturgy. I propose that this should also include the liturgy after the liturgy. Angry preaching should be heard in the workplace, on the streets, in the townships, and in the marketplace. The anger of postcolonial preaching should not stay in the place of worship but should take hold everywhere the church is present.

What I have been trying to propose in the rhetoric of postcolonial preaching is, in essence, the rhetoric of being human. Of speaking as we are. Of preaching not with the voice of religiosity, but with human voices, within human experiences of suffering, struggle, and survival. Postcolonial rhetoric is the secularization of Christian rhetoric and in that sense the revival of human words.

> In short, for us, being Christian means to be truly human rather than being religious in any narrow sense of that word; it also means striving to become more fully human in solidarity with the rest of humankind in the struggle for a more humane, just and peaceable world that respects human dignity and freedom, as well as the integrity of creation.[32]

In a rhetoric of struggle, foolishness, and anger, the point of relation is being human, speaking as human beings within the contextual realities of our world, as we are: angry, struggling fools. At the same time, postcolonial preaching is not about already having arrived but, as de Gruchy rightly says, "striving to become more fully human." The postcolonial preacher

---

30. McKaiser, *Run Racist Run*, 9–10.
31. Wepener and Pieterse, "Angry Preaching," 415.
32. De Gruchy, "Christian Humanism," 57–58.

strives through her rhetoric of struggle and foolishness to become more articulate of the human condition, to speak more clearly against the irrational myths, to call more clearly for a decolonization of the mind, to preach more certainly the good news for the disenfranchised, decentered, and fragmentation reality of existence.

Adam Neder proposes that following Christ is "the summons to discipleship [as] a summons to live with the grain of one's identity in Christ rather than against it."[33] If our identity is inherently decentered and fragmented, this would mean living into the contingency of our existence amongst others in every sense, neither inferior nor superior, but struggling fools who learn to cooperate with one another as well as we possibly can.

Once more, the rhetoric of humanity for postcolonial preaching is the rediscovery of our shared humanity and the terms by which all of us, irrespective of our location of culture or even our faith, or lack thereof, can be united in this shared humanity.

POSTCOLONIAL PREACHING: A PRELIMINARY DEFINITION

In Johan Cilliers' contemplation on a working theory for preaching, he claims four voices as paramount for preaching: God's voice, the text's voice, the congregation's voice, and the preacher's voice.

> Preaching takes place when God's voice is heard through the voice of the text, in the voice of the time (congregational context), through the (unique) voice of the preacher. When these four voices become one voice, then the sermon is indeed viva vox evangelii.[34]

Postcolonial preaching will consider these four voices as follows. One, God's voice as subject to a postcolonial identity, fragmented and decentered. Two, the text's voice as imagining a decolonization of the mind. Three, the congregation's voice as a contextual locality of the struggle for life. And four, the preacher's voice as open to the interaction of many legitimate centers.

---

33. Neder, *Theology as a Way of Life*, 26.
34. Cilliers, *Living Voice of the Gospel*, 32.

On God

> 1. Preaching is the Word of God which he himself speaks, claiming for the purpose the exposition of a biblical text in free human words that are relevant to contemporaries by those who are called to do this in the church that is obedient to its commission.
>
> 2. Preaching is the attempt enjoining upon the church to serve God's own Word, through one who is called thereto, by expounding a biblical text in human words and making it relevant to contemporaries in intimation of what they have to hear from God himself. —Karl Barth[35]

From this definition of preaching, Barth contemplates the following aspects of the definition: revelation, the church, confession, ministry, heralding, scripture, originality, the congregation, and spirituality. Barth's proposal for preaching is thus more extensive than that which Johan Cilliers has laid on the table. For instance, Barth distinguished between the church and the congregation; the first being the event where the sacraments and preaching come together to conform to revelation.[36] And the latter is the contextual situation of the congregation, including "a feeling for *Kairos*."[37]

Returning to Barth's definition of preaching in conversation with postcolonial thought, some crucial aspects must be underscored. One, Barth's conviction that revelation comes from an external divine source must be questioned. Two, postcolonial preaching must ask about interlocutors and the location of interpretation in the exposition of a biblical text. Three, Barth's insistence on "relevance to contemporaries" should be underscored, but with the condition that the postcolonial identity is understood as decentered and fragmented. At the same time, Barth's proposal that the preacher has to have "a feeling for the *Kairos*" of the context should be underscored.

Unlike Barth's perspective, postcolonial homiletics cannot rely justifiably on a divine source of revelation. This does not mean that postcolonial homiletics cannot say anything about God or cannot believe in God. On the contrary, a postcolonial faith can undoubtedly speak about God from a centered perspective without nullifying other ways of talking about God.

---

35. Barth, *Homiletics*, 44.
36. Barth, *Homiletics*, 56–57.
37. Barth, *Homiletics*, 84–85.

Ishmael Tetteh can be found in what I believe is a strong postcolonial and African movement regarding the center of revelation. When Tetteh contemplates who God is, he deconstructs seven beliefs about God. These are: 1) that God is the God of a sect who rejects people of all other sects; 2) that God is a judgmental God whose anger flares more than that of humans and who has created a place called hell; 3) that God is a semi-powerful God with a nemesis who can contest God for the souls of people; 4) that God is a gendered God who prefers one gender above another; 5) that God is a remote-controlled God who exists far away from the world yet controls what happens in the world; 6) that God is a racial God who prefers one race of people, and their culture, above others; 7) that God is a bloodthirsty God who requires the sacrifice of his only Son for the forgiveness of humanity's sin.[38]

I propose that these rejections about God Tetteh propose are rejections of a Western-centered view of God, or rather, a colonial view of God. However, the postcolonial task is not yet done; after the deconstruction of the location of revelation, Tetteh places the following interpretation of God on the table:

> This "God" is the very energy of life, present in all things as the substance of all things. He [sic] is a Father-Mother God, balanced as the polarity of sexes. He-She embodies the entire universe as its substance, energy, law and cohesive love. All things dwell and have their existence in Him-Her. He-She is the only power, wisdom and presence there is. This is my God.[39]

This is, after all, merely an example of perceiving God differently because of another center of perspective. Once more, Tetteh's proposal cannot become the new center. Thus, a postcolonial understanding of preaching will open new spaces of negotiation for an understanding of revelation and God's being. Other ways of thinking about who God is should be welcomed with open arms by the postcolonial preacher. However, all ideas about God which promote the irrational myth, the colonization of the mind, and absolute ways of perceiving and living in the world should be rejected.

In postcolonial preaching, God becomes the one with many faces, whereby God is liberated from possessing one center of thinking towards many potential encounters with God in the faces of people, like and unlike

---

38. Tetteh, *Fountain of Life*, 34.
39. Tetteh, *Fountain of Life*, 35.

us.[40] Cas Wepener proposes that some biblical texts on what God does and who God is, showcase God as robust in the sense of un-possessable, hard to handle, and queer in identity.[41] In postcolonial preaching, God can move beyond our definitions of order, clean, correct, and regular. Nancy Eiesland speaks of God in the following way, "in a sip-puff wheelchair. . . . Not an omnipotent, self-sufficient God, but neither a pitiable, suffering servant. . . . I beheld God as a survivor, unpitying and forthright."[42]

The point is clear: postcolonial preaching, in its source of revelation, in its articulation of the divine, and in its relationship with other ways of interpreting revelation, is an endeavor of decentering interpretation and articulation without absolutizing a particular perspective.

On the Text

> I would portray postcolonial preaching as a locally rooted and globally conscious performance that seeks to create a Third Space so that the faith community can imagine new ways of being in the world and encountering God's salvific action for the oppressed and marginalized. —KWOK PUI-LAN[43]

As a point of reference for the voice of the text as imagining a decolonized consciousness, let us consider Hans Leander's thoughts on Mark 11:1–11. From the very beginning of his contemplation, Leander understands that the political nature of Jesus' entry into Jerusalem must be interpreted concerning Roman imperialism.[44] At the same time, he adequately articulates his suspicion that biblical scholars who exclude this relationship to Roman imperialism do so because of their "social location."[45] In this sense, he first contemplates the commentary of Ezra Gould, whose location of culture is that of Britain in the late nineteenth century. What Leander finds in Gould's interpretation is rather lurid:

> The Protestant identity formation, of which Gould's interpretation was a part, was somewhat contradictory. On the one hand, it could be characterized as non-worldly and non-political. On the

---

40. Kearney and Kavanagh, "Interview with Richard Kearney," 4.
41. Wepener, "Gay-Gesprek."
42. Eiesland, *Disabled God*, 89.
43. Pui-lan, "Postcolonial Preaching in Intercultural Contexts," 11.
44. Leander, "With Homi Bhabha," 309.
45. Leander, "With Homi Bhabha," 310.

POSTCOLONIAL PREACHING?

other hand, it was part of a social practice (Christian mission) that both legitimized and resisted a highly political and worldly colonial expansion. Despite the complexity of its discursive location, however, Gould's image of a "purely spiritual Jesus" that does not interfere with the state could quite clearly be labeled pro-colonial and acquiescent.[46]

Gould, as interlocutor, is thus an antagonist in contemplating the interpretation of the text in a postcolonial fashion. However, he is not the only one. Leander also considers the insights of Richard Horsley. Leander finds that Horsley represents an anti-colonial stance, where Jesus stands with the people in opposition to the rulers, aiming for political liberation. Leander concludes with the following about Horsley:

> In my final reading of Horsley, therefore, his interpretation of Mark quite clearly represents a typical anti-colonial position. . . . Although an anti-colonial reading such as Horsley's could be appreciated as a challenge to the comfortable, acquiescent readings of Mark, it nevertheless lacks tools for accentuating the subtlety and complexity that I will argue is typical of Mark's way of reinscribing and subverting Roman power.[47]

As a postcolonial endeavor, Leander's interpretation of Mark 11:1–11 takes cognizance that triumphal entries were quite common in the ancient world. However, what distinguished Jesus' entry into Jerusalem in Mark 11:1–11 is the end of the pericope. Usually, processions of entry end in a ritual at the temple. However, in Mark 11:11, there is an anti-climax: "when [Jesus] had looked around at everything, as it was already late, he went out to Bethany with the twelve."[48] In conversation with Homi Bhabha, Leander understands the anti-climax at the end as mimicry: "a parodic undermining of imperial notions of power."[49] This parodic mimicry thus opens an imaginative negotiation of meaning and future potential, undermining both a triumphant kingship and militant revolt. Leander concludes:

> The profound threat to imperial hegemony does not lie then, as one would perhaps assume, in an oppositional contrasting of the Lord Jesus and the Lord Emperor, but rather in the somewhat

---

46. Leander, "With Homi Bhabha," 314.
47. Leander, "With Homi Bhabha," 317.
48. Mark 11:11, ESV.
49. Leander, "With Homi Bhabha," 323.

playful and ambivalent subversions of its very notions of strength and triumph.[50]

The creative potential of the text of decolonization of the mind lies precisely in this creative endeavor of neither colonial authoritarianism nor a blind revolution that seeks to overthrow all things no matter the costs or consequences.

On the Context

> [The colonial] worldview of opposing and antagonistic binaries . . . continues to hurt both colonizers and colonized peoples by keeping them divided and engaged in cycles of oppression. —LIS VALLE[51]

During apartheid, Black Theology of Liberation (BTL) was at the forefront and cutting edge of interpreting the Kairos of the moment. With this, I mean that BTL could concretely name the social, political, and economic injustices intertwined with apartheid. As Sizwe shows, the apartheid government is "guilty of tyranny, when it denies human rights to some of its people."[52] Similarly, Mofokeng critiqued the capitalist system of apartheid as "surplus extraction at the expense of workers here and abroad."[53] So, the Confession of Belhar rejects the apartheid ideology "which [legitimates] forms of injustice."[54] This is not to say that everyone agreed that apartheid was against the gospel. Allan Boesak's contemplation on the theological interpretation of apartheid showcases white theologians for (Koot Vorster) and against (Beyers Naudé) apartheid, as well as the black church's underlying white theology, which did not question apartheid and the theological struggle against apartheid within the black church.[55]

However, since democracy, and maybe because of the perception that democracy brings justice, the feeling for Kairos dissipated. Firstly, prominent theologians of BTL during apartheid were absorbed into

---

50. Leander, "With Homi Bhabha," 330.
51. Valle, "Toward Postcolonial Liturgical Preaching," 28.
52. Sizwe, "Christian's Political Responsibility," 50.
53. Mofokeng, "Cross in the Search," 46.
54. "Confession of Belhar," 2.
55. Boesak, *Kairos, Crisis, and Global Apartheid*, 40.

administrative positions in the new democratic government.[56] Secondly, constitutional democracy as national liberation was understood as the gateway to addressing all forms of injustice in South Africa.[57] And thirdly, the church saw national liberation as the opportunity to return to the so-called real work of the church, the spiritual and moral guidance of the faithful.[58] A fourth reason for the lack of Kairos is not so much the mistiming of Kairos but the importance the prosperity gospel had started playing in politics since 1994.[59] During the presidency of Jacob Zuma, the National Interfaith Leadership Council (NILC), led by the televangelist Ray McCauley, played a central role in advising the president. During this same time, the South African Council of Churches (SACC) publicly criticized the governing party's corruption but was side-lined by Zuma.[60] The combination of these reasons made it impossible for BTL to engage in continuous and pioneering analysis of the new struggles in democratic South Africa.

At the same time, some stood firm or instead reiterated the insights of BTL as espoused during apartheid. In my opinion, Allan Boesak is the forerunner of this movement. In his writing and sermons since democracy (more accurately, since the end of his political career), he has been adamant that nothing has changed, that apartheid, although supposedly over, is everywhere, alive and well.[61] On the one hand, Boesak claims an acute feeling for Kairos:

> In the global community today we are facing serious challenges across the world in terms of our constitutional democracies, political integrity, spiritual authenticity, political moral authority, and our prophetic faithfulness. In our day, in our presence, struggles for justice, freedom, human dignity, and the integrity of creation are sweeping across the globe.[62]

I have much regard for Boesak's insistence and feel for Kairos. However, I am unconvinced of his underlying hermeneutics. I think Boesak is merely anti-colonial. His feeling for Kairos brings him to repeat the insights of BTL during apartheid, that hermeneutic privilege should be given to

---

56. Maluleke, "Black and African Theology," 194.
57. Dolamo, "Does Black Theology Have a Role?," 44.
58. Boesak, *Running with Horses*, 8.
59. Boesak, *Dare We Speak of Hope?*, 55–56.
60. Pillay, "Faith and Reality," 4.
61. See Wessels, "Contemplating Allan Boesak's Fascination."
62. Boesak, *Kairos, Crisis, and Global Apartheid*, 92.

the location of culture of the subaltern and that this hermeneutical positionality is the normative and correct place of God's justice. However, his relation to other centers is a mere oppositionality thereof. Other centers of thought are merely unjust and should be rejected. Furthermore, he does not question how much of an influence an anti-colonial stance has had and may still have in epistemological repetition and strengthening of colonial sentiments, which divide people, rather than present the possibility of cooperation.

Lis Valle proposes an entirely different approach. She is acutely aware of the injustices still prevalent in the colonial worldview "of opposing and antagonistic binaries."[63] However, instead of repeating those oppositions from an anti-colonial position, she proposes "a worldview of 'complementary dualities.'"[64] In this proposal, the colonizer and the colonized are not seen as opposites—the one to be overcome, subjugated, or even killed; and the other the bearer of truth and justice—depending on your perspective. Both are understood as kept divided by the colonial worldview and trapped in cycles of oppression.

Aimé Césaire concurs with this understanding, stating that colonization has been detrimental to the minds of the colonized and has brutalized the colonizer, dehumanized them, and alienated them from the common humanity.[65] A feeling for Kairos as a postcolonial practice is a feeling for the methods and means of transcending the dualities of the colonial myth. Valle goes on to propose that a worldview of complementary dualities means: "In short, opposites need, constitute, and complement each other."[66] For Valle, postcolonial preaching is a journey of proclaiming imagined fragments of "a completely different reality, a different way of being in the world, and of relating to each other."[67] This imagination is not governed by colonization nor anti-colonial sentiments but transcends the colonial dualities towards complementarity. In this sense, one could argue that to imagine the context correctly would include disregarding the attitude which sees our world only as competing factions but potentially as beings who must cooperate in the struggle for life. Stated differently, through this complementarity of dualities, the possibility of negotiated space breaks open where colonized

63. Valle, "Toward Postcolonial Liturgical Preaching," 28.
64. Valle, "Toward Postcolonial Liturgical Preaching," 28.
65. Césaire, *Discourse on Colonialism*, 41.
66. Valle, "Toward Postcolonial Liturgical Preaching," 30.
67. Valle, "Toward Postcolonial Liturgical Preaching," 32.

and colonizer, and identities which could not so easily be camped as either, can be what they indeed are; equal and dignified human beings who seek and work together. Valle's point:

> There is something else, something that the community must build using the prophetic imagination of prophets in the Old Testament and of current theologians, in addition to their own.[68]

At the same time, a feeling for Kairos cannot ignore the economic realities. Fanon convincingly proposed that land is an issue in the African context. For Fanon, the land is not only about sustenance but dignity.[69] And without dignity and trust in oneself and the greater community, what sustainable economy is possible? Furthermore, the land is a contentious issue in South Africa, with a clear indication that the ANC and the president, Cyril Ramaphosa, have been pushing for land expropriation since 2020:

> We're calling for the amendment of section 25 of the constitution, and it was agreed that the ANC must embark on an intensive programme to popularize and explain its position on the amendment. The lekgotla endorsed that the power related to issues of expropriation of land without compensation should reside in the executive.[70]

However, and this is where the postcolonial interpretation of Kairos comes into play, should the land issue not be a conversation on human well-being? Should there not be an imagination of alternatives rather than the duality of expropriation of land, which merely takes from the one and gives to the other? And who receives land? Or is land expropriation merely a façade whereby the political elite monopolize land? But, also, can we imagine different economies? And different ways of economic relations in South Africa, other than the racially clouded dualism inherited from colonization and apartheid?

At the same time, a postcolonial feeling for Kairos might determine that economies do not develop from the top down. Neither are economies independent from human relations, everyday struggles, and our bodies. Wa Thiong'o's call for "national, democratic and human liberation" is a call for struggle both in understanding the intricate workings of our time

---

68. Valle, "Toward Postcolonial Liturgical Preaching," 32.
69. Fanon, *Wretched of the Earth*, 9.
70. Pres. Cyril Ramaphosa during the ANC lekgotla of 2020, as quoted by Bhengu, "ANC Lekgotla Outcomes," para. 7.

and calling for the imagination of linguistic, mental, and physical struggle against the irrational myth of authoritarianism, even when found in new garb in the contemporary context.[71] It is naming contemporary sites of struggle and imagining fragments of a different world by which humankind can be united in the struggle for liberation from authoritarian structures. For Harvey Cox, kerygma is "the language of specific announcements about where the work of liberation is now proceeding and concrete invitations to join in the struggle."[72] He goes on to show that certain powers govern the world, powers against which must be struggled and that the Christian in the secular, postcolonial age must be a person who takes responsibility "in and for the city of man, or become once again a slave to dehumanizing powers."[73]

Locating the struggle for life through valid contextual interpretation is paramount to postcolonial preaching.

On the Preacher

> But it did point out the possibility of moving the center from its location in Europe towards a pluralism of centers; themselves being equally legitimate locations of the human imagination. —Ngũgĩ wa Thiong'o[74]

Consider momentarily that the postcolonial preacher will not be the harbinger of either a colonial and authoritarian word or an activist and revolutionary idealist. Instead, here arises the possibility of a person who moves between and betwixt ideological and hermeneutic centers. A person who can wisely traverse the tribal and polarizing tendencies of a context relentlessly underscored by such impetuses.

Postcolonial Preaching Defined

And thus, I now turn to a preliminary definition of postcolonial preaching.

Postcolonial preaching takes place when the fragmented and decentered God speaks through the biblical text, which neither underscores

---

71. Wa Thiong'o, *Decolonising the Mind*, 108.
72. Cox, *Secular City*, 151.
73. Cox, *Secular City*, 152–54, 157.
74. Wa Thiong'o, *Moving the Centre*, 26.

authoritarian control nor revolutionary impulses, but a decolonization of the mind for a people who find themselves in a struggle for life by the human endeavor of a preacher intent on moving between the ideological centers of a tribal world. Postcolonial preaching is the attempt by a human, in relation to other humans, to conceptualize the biblical text as a decolonial force of consciousness in a cooperative attempt to struggle for life, as spoken by a God whose face constantly alludes us.

AN ATTEMPT[75] AT A POSTCOLONIAL SERMON

Arise, shine, for . . . the stranger has come.

January 5, 2020 (Second Sunday after Christmas Day)[76]

Isa 60:1–6
Ps 72:1–5

Someone once said that to leave home and to return is a comedy, but when we do not return, it is a tragedy. No one leaves home if they do not need to. We leave home only when forced, when economic, political, or personal reasons coerce us. When returning, whatever happened, whatever sorrow, whatever pain, it is all gone. It is a comedy. But when you do not return home, it is a tragedy.

I

You have heard, and our text witnesses again today: "Shine your light!" These words are nothing new to us. In a sense, it has already been spoken

---

75. I choose to speak of an attempt, as I am convinced that postcolonial preaching is never a completed endeavor. Neither is this sermon without its shortcomings and colonial discourse. At the same time, I have tried to keep as close to the verbatim expression (albeit translated from Afrikaans to English) as I used it during the sermon. I have also chosen not to interpret the sermon, but to leave it open to interpretation of its postcolonial consciousness (or lack thereof).

76. This sermon was preached on January 5, 2020 at the Soutpan Dutch Reformed Church in the Free State, South Africa. It is my opinion that the congregation is, on the one hand, disenfranchised because of their location of culture in a very rural area of the Free State. The membership is minimal. At the same time, the members are all white and Afrikaans, and the system of thought is that of Afrikaner Nationalism. When I spoke to some of the members before the worship service, there was a strong feeling of both sadness because of the small membership, and resentment of people who are of different cultures/races. The sermon was preached in Afrikaans, and this version is a translation afterward.

many times, and we have heard it many times, in many forms throughout generations. To Abraham, God said, "I will bless you . . . so that you will be a blessing."[77] This was a calling of the public being to the inclusion of others. To Israel, in words we hear today, "Arise, shine, for your light has come." In other words, after the night of exile comes the light of the Lord's glory, and Israel is called to shine that light. We have heard these words for the disciples: "in the same way, let your light shine before others."[78] These words were given to the disciples and the church, and also to us, "Let your light shine!"

And it is correct what we have heard; that we must live our lives in such a way, in an ethical way, so that those who see what we do will see our good works and give praise to God. We should be the people who exist differently in this world.

II

However, Isa 60, this morning, does not speak about *our* light. It does not talk about the light as our good works. No. The light in our text is "the glory of the Lord [which] has risen upon you." During certain times, from the perspective of the faithful, the Lord's glory was nowhere to be found. But now, it has arisen. Now it is Emmanuel, God with Us. Now, it is the child in the manger who has come. Now the Lord's glory is here and must be shone to the world!

Who is this child, born not in Medi-Clinic, Rose Park Hospital, or Pelonomi Hospital? Who is this child born in the equivalent of someone's garage? Is he the light? Is he the glory of the Lord's presence? Let's think about this together. He is not born in a place of power, yet he is the expected king. He does not live in comfort, yet he brings peace and well-being. He does not lead a revolution, yet his kingdom has come.

If this child is the glory of God's presence, then the shining of our light is to point to this child, to proclaim him and what he has done. It is to point to what he did and said. His first sermon was this: "Repent, for the kingdom of heaven is at hand."[79] And today we have heard of the king in Ps 72: the defender of the cause of the poor, the deliverer of the children of the needy, the crusher of the oppressed. All these words are political, and we must hear them this way. This child, this man from the poor Nazareth, this

---

77. Gen 12:2, ESV.
78. Matt 5:16, ESV.
79. Matt 4:17, ESV.

man amongst the oppressed, is the king of a new kingdom, a new politic, a new economy, a new society.

Put another way; there is a place of righteousness and justice. There is a kingdom of equality, and for all to have enough. There is a city, a republic, and a society that includes and welcomes. The aggrieved, the widow, the orphan, the stranger, and us; are all welcome.

Let your light shine! This light.

III

But a question we seldom ask is: What happens when this light is shone into the world? "And nations shall come to your light, and kings to the brightness of your rising."

Imagine that. But in reality, no imagination is necessary. This is very normal. To be drawn to light is very normal, very human. And in our text, people from all nations come "to your light." To this place. To the site where the king is proclaimed. To the kingdom which is different from the kingdoms of our world; different to the places of injustice, of selfishness, of economies of abuse, and of politics of violence.

Again, strangers come to the light: people of different cultures and people of different languages. *The other* comes to the light.

Let's be honest with ourselves, we, the Afrikaners. We are not very good when it comes to strangers. We struggle to welcome those who look different. We struggle to have relationships with those who believe differently, speak differently, and smell differently. We struggle with those who love differently. With those who worship differently.

But, if we take our text seriously, God loves diversity. God welcomes diversity. To let our light shine is also to welcome the stranger. To let our light shine is to sit with the other at the communion table. Not so we can change them to become like us. But just to sit with them as they are, strangers.

To let our light shine is to let the stranger be themselves. The stranger comes to the shining light as they are; with their abundance and wealth. This wealth is, first of all, economic wealth but it is also more than that; it is a cultural abundance. Stated differently, the stranger comes with the abundance of their language, worldview, religion, and how they think, believe, do, and live.

And it is at this moment, not before, but when the stranger has come with all she has, that *they* "shall bring good news, the praises of the Lord."[80]

In other terms, we cannot praise God and enjoy God all the days of our lives on our own. We cannot shine our light alone, but only once the stranger has come, with the stranger amongst us.

IV

To leave home and to return is a comedy. To leave home and never return is a tragedy. As the faithful, we understand and believe that to be in the presence of the Lord is the grand homecoming. To enter the kingdom of Heaven, the house of the Lord, the new Jerusalem.

However, if it is a tragedy when we do not return home, what is it if we are excluded from the house of the Lord just as we stand at the entrance? What is it if we are excluded because of who we are or where we live? Is that not the epitome of tragedy?

May we shine our light! And may we keep the doors of the Lord's kingdom open.

Amen.

---

80. Isa 60:6, ESV.

Chapter 3

Postcolonial Liturgical Contemplation

> Liturgies are powerful actions that tell us what and how to think, what (not) to do, how and what (not) to relate to, what to avoid, and so on. Liturgical religious movements shape bodies, minds, spirits, politics, economies, and nation-states. —Cláudio Carvalhaes[1]

IN THIS BOOK, I have endeavored to define postcolonial preaching. However, the sermon does not stand alone.[2] No sermon is preached without the accompaniment of some sort of liturgical movement. Even the complete absence of liturgy has liturgical implications. And no liturgical action is without its impact on shaping how people interact and live with each other in this world. As Cláudio Carvalhaes acutely proposes, liturgy within the faith community impacts the whole of human existence.

Walter Mignolo has opined that a decolonial consciousness brings forth other ways of understanding, thinking, relating, and existing in this world, politically and economically.[3] Thus, just as preaching is part and parcel of the worship service, part of the liturgy of the faith community, so too must this book contemplate the implications of postcolonial thought for the whole of the worship service. Once more, when doing homiletics, I also want to busy myself with the liturgy. When contemplating postcolonial thought for preaching and the homiletic community, I, too, must consider postcolonial thought for the liturgy.

---

1. Carvalhaes, "Liturgy and Postcolonialism," 3.
2. See Wepener and Klomp, "Verhouding Prediking."
3. Mignolo, "Delinking," 452–53.

Put another way, to my mind, a chapter on liturgy within this book is wholly justified. How we worship transcends the confines of the Service of the Word and takes place in the whole liturgical experience. The liturgy precedes the Service of the Word, and the latter is part and parcel of the former. Furthermore, the worship service continues into the world, the liturgy after the liturgy.

For my contemplation on postcolonial liturgical practice, I will interlock with the three focal images I delimited in chapter 1: The irrational myth and the decolonization of the mind; moving the center; and a decentred, fragmented identity. The last two focal images will be contemplated together. At the same time, Mignolo's insistence that the postcolonial "struggle is for changing the terms in addition to the content of the conversation" must be considered.[4]

IRRATIONAL MYTHS AND THE LITURGY

> At its heart, liturgical/ritual dynamics are deeply related to power, either maintaining or opposing powers already in place. Whoever holds religious power defines, allows, authorizes, and demands the proper practices/behaviors of the faith—a flight from the first liturgical sense of the *work of the people* to the work of specialists done *on behalf of the people*. —Cláudio Carvalhaes[5]

From a postcolonial perspective, as Carvalhaes indicates, liturgy must be considered within the framework of power relations. In chapter 1, I delimited the overarching power structure of the postcolony as the irrational myths embedded in global capitalism and counter-movements. However, before turning to the relationship between the irrational myths and liturgy in the contemporary context, a short historical reflection between liturgy and power within the broader societal context is necessary.

> The leadership of the church in the fourth century realized that the church had to transform the values of Roman society. Liturgy was one of the means by which the values of the kingdom of God would be proclaimed and expressed in preaching and sacramental celebration.[6]

---

4. Mignolo, "Delinking," 459.
5. Carvalhaes, "Liturgy and Postcolonialism," 4.
6. Senn, *People's Work*, 42.

Postcolonial Liturgical Contemplation

After the Christian religion became a legal cult in the Roman Empire during the fourth century, as Frank Senn adeptly shows, the liturgy played a fundamental role in the attempt at transforming society towards the understanding of life per the kingdom of God. In a sense, the power dynamic at that time was, for the first time in Christian history, at such a juncture that an endeavor of liturgy as part and parcel of political life could take place. However, as Brad Gregory reasons, by the late Middle Ages, the idea that the church could transform society towards the kingdom of God "fell gravely short" of being realized.[7]

Stated otherwise, as much as the church was in a position of power, attempts to bring about God's kingdom did not pan out because of the "widespread failures of secular and ecclesiastical authorities to find nonoppressive ways of exercising power consistent with *caritas*."[8] It was at this juncture that the Reformation took place, however, bringing with it a twofold complexification of the problem of bringing the kingdom of God in any real-world terms:

> The unintended problem created by the Reformation was therefore not simply a perpetuation of the inherited and still-present challenge of how to make human life more genuinely Christian, but also the new and compounding problem of how to know what true Christianity was. "Scripture alone" was not a solution to this new problem, but its cause.[9]

Gregory proposes that the solution for this unintended problem bought on by the Reformation came to the fore through the Dutch Republic:

> Especially in the maritime and mercantile province of Holland, a distinction was in effect being drawn between public and private life, and "religion"—understood largely as a matter of belief, worship, and devotion—was being individualized, privatized, and separated from political and economic life. So long as one obeyed the laws that provided for common security and stability, one could believe whatever one wished and worship in private however one pleased.[10]

---

7. Gregory, *Unintended Reformation*, 367.
8. Gregory, *Unintended Reformation*, 367.
9. Gregory, *Unintended Reformation*, 368–69.
10. Gregory, *Unintended Reformation*, 373–74.

If Gregory is correct, the privatization of worship has had an immense influence on the power dynamic between the church as the herald of the gospel and the political implications of the gospel. Herein the lived experience is colonized by proposing body and spirit, economy and church, life and religion have nothing to do with each other. In this line of thought, Carvalhaes' proposal that liturgies "are powerful actions" which inform our very existence in this world, personally and politically, seems a bit far-fetched. After all, if liturgy is merely private and has nothing to do with public life, how can it have any power in shaping civic life? Has privatization trumped the political and social implications of the liturgy even before the service has started?

Yet, Carvalhaes is not alone in proposing that liturgy profoundly influences human existence in the world. In like manner, James Smith is convinced that liturgy recruits "hearts and minds of the people of God" for public participation in bearing God's image within the world for the benefit of all creation.[11] However, how has this mission of the church played out in the real world?

In the South African context, the Dutch Reformed Church (DRC), convinced of their understanding of the gospel and the implications thereof for the wider society, endorsed apartheid in 1949:

> In 1949, the Cape DRC synod gave a slightly more circumspect endorsement of apartheid. Its main argument was based on historical precedents. It referred to the 1857 DRC synod decision to condone segregated worship, to the segregation of schools, and to the church's mission policy laid down in 1935. Apartheid, the synod declared, did not mean oppression or black inferiority but a "vertical separation" in which each population group could become independent. As Richard Elphick remarks, the church leaders were enthralled by their utopian vision of separate people, each with their own mission, and would continue to justify the unjustifiable, thus paving the way for the politicians.[12]

It is interesting to note Giliomee's last sentence, "paving the way for the politicians." This implies that the political institutions of the day were willing to justify governmental policies by showcasing that the church underscores such policies. Thus, from a political point of view, the church did not influence society on the church's terms, nor did the South African

---

11. Smith, *Imagining the Kingdom*, 151.
12. Giliomee, "Making of the Apartheid Plan," 383–84.

context of the late twentieth century have a complete privatization of religion. However, the influence of the DRC's choice to separate the Lord's Supper on the grounds of the "weakness of some"[13] certainly impacted the greater social landscape of society. Thus, rather than complete privatization or a thorough public mission of the church, the church's influence in society is on an ad hoc basis, but not to the extent of a transformation of societal values.

At the same time, the example of apartheid could showcase the exact opposite. It could be that the liturgical separation of people in 1857 was not based on Christian liturgy but on the greater colonial worldview and culture of the time.[14] Then, it was not the liturgy that shaped society, but instead, society shaping liturgy. In this instance, the liturgy seems only later to justify the injustice of apartheid. Most likely, it is both culture that has an influence on cult, and cult which influences culture.

Important questions thus arise. What influence do the irrational myths have on and within Christian worship today?

I propose three ways in which the irrational myths (lex norma vivendi[15]) shape the liturgy (lex orandi) today: 1) authoritarianism, 2) polarization, and 3) parody.

Authoritarianism

> In every society the production of discourse is at once controlled, selected, organised and redistributed . . . In a society like ours, the procedures of exclusion are well known. The most obvious and familiar is the prohibition. We know quite well that we do not have the rights to say everything, that we cannot speak of just anything in any circumstances whatever, and that not everyone has the right to speak of anything whatever. —MICHEL FOUCAULT[16]

---

13. See Wepener, "Still Because of the Weakness?"

14. In James Smith's contemplation between the relationship culture and liturgy, he opines that culture's influence on liturgy is always present and vice versa. However, he insists that there should be "an ecclesial center of gravity" with regards to the interaction. See Smith, *Desiring the Kingdom*, 36.

15. By changing the oft-used concept of *lex vivendi* to *lex norma vivendi*, I am proposing that there should be a differentiation between the law of living (which could be many laws of living) to the normative center which the irrational myth deems itself to be—thus *the obliged law of living*.

16. Foucault, "Order of Discourse," 52.

POSTCOLONIAL HOMILETICS?

Michel Foucault proposes that discourse, and thus discourse in the liturgy, is ordered by what is excluded and prohibited. Foucault suggests that the themes most tightly controlled by the social system of thought are politics and sexuality. Unfortunately, the scope of this book does not include contemplation on sexuality and liturgy, although I suspect a prohibition on sexual discourse within the liturgy is indeed prominent. Regarding politics, I am convinced that speech is prohibited and directed toward what fits into the conceptual framework of irrational myths.

In a recent second-year university class about Jesus' proclamation of the Jubilee, I was not surprised to hear that the students were unaware that the confession *Jesus is Lord* is political. In the discussion, I asked about the meaning of this confession. The students all claimed that this confession meant personal lordship over their hearts and lifestyles. The implication was that only those who have faith in Jesus are under his lordship. Yet, the confession *Jesus is Lord* speaks of the political implications of Jesus as Lord, King, and President over all of life, whether faith is involved or not.[17] In this line of thought, leaders of all nations are under the dominion of Jesus.

As a case in point between the political content present and the prohibition of discourse on political content in the liturgy, I will look at the Confession of Belhar. Dirkie Smit explains that the Confession of Belhar was born in a historical moment of need for adequate gospel proclamation given the sociopolitical context of apartheid.[18] Thus, the Confession of Belhar came to the fore. And it confessed within the societal context of justification of apartheid by the DRC. Yet, as Smit points out, the theological truths of the Confession of Belhar transcend the historical context in which it was born to speak, often surprisingly, in new settings.[19]

Smit shows that the introduction of the Confession of Belhar had already laid the political implications for the church, that the church is understood not in coalition with or loyalty to the political ideology of apartheid,[20] but political allegiance with the reign of Jesus Christ.[21] This allegiance with Christ's reign is identified through three focal images: unity, reconciliation, and justice.

---

17. Boesak, *Tenderness of Conscience*, 142.
18. Smit, "Oor die Teologiese Inhoud," 186.
19. Smit, "Oor die Teologiese Inhoud," 187.
20. By implication, not in coalition with any political ideology of any time or place.
21. Smit, "Oor die Teologiese Inhoud," 189.

Regarding unity, Smit opines that Belhar implies the unity of the church to be visible.[22] Thus, instead of apartheid's political system of separation of people, Belhar calls for the inclusion of diversity and such inclusion in a visible manner. This has political implications for a world of separation. Today, this separation of people finds new forms in authoritarian claims on both the extreme right, which find expression in racism, and the extreme left, which claims racial victimhood and the need for authoritarian sanctioned and controlled equality of outcome.

Concerning reconciliation, Smit proposes that Belhar calls for reconciliation to be played out in history, realized, practiced, and embodied.[23] This, once more, is what constitutes the political: the embodiment of ideals within the polis. Lastly, about justice, Smit first shows how justice is something that God does. It is the biblical God who brings justice to those who experience injustice. It is this God who helps those who are without help. This God is faithful to the covenant, upholding his love and promises. It is this God who sees and who saves us from sin and suffering. This God stands next to the suffering, the poor, and the aggrieved. And this God calls his church to follow in this endeavor of justice.[24] This is the third political imperative of Belhar. Smit goes on to say:

> The church belonging to this God is called to stand where this God stands. This means that the church will witness against injustice and against all the powerful who selfishly search purely for their interests even though these actions are disadvantaging others.[25]

This, I propose, is the political imperative of the Confession of Belhar for the liturgy *par excellence*: the witness against injustice, the witness against the powerful who pursue an authoritarian regime irrelevant to the well-being of the people.

However, as Martin Laubscher correctly shows, Belhar is "underplayed and underdeveloped . . . in the church's worship and liturgy."[26] Once more, in my opinion, the liturgical discourse does not allow Belhar to be articulated, or when indeed articulated, to be taken seriously for its political implications.

---

22. Smit, "Oor die Teologiese Inhoud," 191.
23. Smit, "Oor die Teologiese Inhoud," 193.
24. Smit, "Oor die Teologiese Inhoud," 193–94.
25. Smit, "Oor die Teologiese Inhoud," 194: my translation.
26. Laubscher, "Belhar, Liturgy and Life?," 2.

Postcolonial Homiletics?

Laubscher shows how liturgy has often followed the status quo: "*the way we lived became the way we believed and eventually the way we prayed.*"[27] Returning to the way liturgy functioned in apartheid, Laubscher determines (in line with Jaap Durand) that the "actual problem with apartheid" was "that it functioned as a theological doctrine (read: heresy) that believed in the irreconcilable nature of humanity."[28] It is without a doubt that Laubscher has a favorable view of the liturgy and the function of the liturgy of worship to influence the liturgy of life.

However, as Laubscher shows, these sentiments are not without an awareness of how Belhar has been marginalized because of a narrow view of theological and baptismal identity within the church.[29] From my anecdotal experience as Minister of Word and Sacrament in the Uniting Reformed Church in Southern Africa (URCSA), I have found that Belhar is also marginal in URCSA's identity, at least at a grassroots level in congregations. Elvis Mofokeng empirically researched the attitude of URCSA members towards the Confession of Belhar and found an ambiguous relationship, ranging from a knowledgeable understanding of Belhar to complete ignorance:

> From the respondents one can notice that the ministers of these congregations are trying to do something about the Belhar Confession by teaching and instilling it in the liturgy. However, there are challenges that the church as a whole need to work on so that the Belhar Confession is taken forward . . . [S]ome of the members ended up thinking that Belhar is the name of a person . . . In both congregations one can notice that church council members have more knowledge [about the Confession of Belhar] than the rest of the church members. That is why one respondent advised that the study should give back a report and provide ways in which young people can also gain better knowledge about the Belhar Confession.[30]

Returning to the earlier statement, I propose that the lack of liturgical identity formation around the Confession of Belhar is founded on the political discourse of Belhar. If my line of thought is accurate, political discourse is quieted and prohibited in a colonial understanding of privatization.

---

27. Laubscher, "Oor die Teologiese Inhoud," 3: original italics.
28. Laubscher, "Oor die Teologiese Inhoud," 3.
29. Laubscher, "Oor die Teologiese Inhoud," 5.
30. Mofokeng, "Belhar Confession and Liturgy," 139.

This idea that the radical intent of speech is subverted, prohibited, quieted, appropriated, and altered is something Allan Boesak finds has happened with the utterances of Desmond Tutu, especially during the Truth and Reconciliation Commission (TRC) years.[31] Boesak says that Tutu's message was always "confession, forgiveness, and reparation."[32] However, because of the distortion of the political implications of reparation, the reception of the TRC, especially amongst white people, ignored the "*capacity of the wrongdoer to make a new beginning on a course that will be different from the one that caused us the wrong.*"[33]

As I have proposed in chapter 1, the irrational myths feed on the ideas of polarization, group identity, stereotypes, and imagined exclusion. John de Gruchy makes the following point:

> My understanding of the church as an inclusive community is contingent precisely on the rejection of false boundaries determined by ethnicity, gender, class or sexual orientation.[34]

The moment of decolonization of the mind comes when the liturgy explicitly breaks down all barriers which exclude. For some, this means being open to welcoming the stranger. For others, this means being welcomed as the stranger. And for all, it means to be open to the dynamics of relating to the other.[35] Liturgically speaking, the breaking of authoritarian insanity lies precisely in the potential inclusion, albeit risky, of a language and imagination that authoritarian insanity does not want. Martin Laubscher proposes an imaginative liturgy using the Confession of Belhar as the source document. I quote only the welcoming:

> Welcome in the name of Jesus Christ! In Christ we share the gift and goal of visible *unity* within the new human community. In Christ we embody *reconciliation* by embracing people who are often socially excluded and exploited. In Christ we practice *justice*

---

31. Boesak, "Subversive Piety," 136.
32. Boesak, "Subversive Piety," 138.
33. Boesak, "Subversive Piety," 136: original italics.
34. De Gruchy, "Christian Humanism," 60.
35. As Miroslav Volf shows, identity formation is dynamic, and we are shaped by the relationships we have with those who are different to us. He goes on to show that an exclusive identity does violence both to the other and to the self. However, he does take cognizance that the embrace of the other should not endanger oneself. Thus, embracing the stranger must be a voluntary action which does not neglect self-care and self-preservation. Volf, "Living with the 'Other,'" 15–23.

by standing where God stands, namely against injustice and with the wronged. To the stranger in need of community, the estranged who longs to embrace the other, and to all who hunger and thirst for justice and righteousness, this congregation opens wide its doors and welcomes all in the name of our Lord, Jesus Christ.[36]

Laubscher's proposal is a movement towards decolonizing the mind through a language that imagines the world not as an authoritarian regime but as open to possibilities of relating with others beyond political control and sanction. Thus, Belhar's postcolonializing potential decolonize the faith community's minds. A world is imagined, and a community is created which rejects tyrannical control's false boundaries.

Polarization

As I wrote this sentence, the University of the Free State and universities around South Africa suspended contact sessions with students because of the worldwide COVID-19 outbreak. This was the beginning of the COVID-19 pandemic. At this early stage of much more to come, two contributions were made in national newspapers regarding virtual worship. The first, by Cas Wepener and Nicolas Matthee. They proposed that virtual liturgies were nothing new and already existed in online gaming and social media.[37] It would stand to reason that virtual worship would be an adequate replacement for weekly gatherings for worship.

Wepener and Matthee refer to how the Spanish Flu transformed Holy Communion. This transformation was the incorporation of small chalices instead of using a communal cup.[38] And indeed, this was an essential and ethically responsible manner of going about the Holy Communion during the Spanish Flu. What interests me, however, is that these small chalices were not dispensed with after the pandemic but continue to be part and parcel of many Reformed churches' worship even today.

The second contribution to this conversation was made by Johann Rossouw, who proposed, from an Orthodox position, that virtual communion is merely an imitation and longing for physical fellowship in a world of liturgical poverty.[39] Interestingly enough, in Matthee's PhD thesis, he partly

36. Laubscher, "Belhar, Liturgy and Life?," 8: original italics.
37. Wepener and Matthee, "Kubernagmaal in Virustyd."
38. Wepener and Matthee, "Kubernagmaal in Virustyd."
39. Rossouw, "Nagmaal Is Nie Sommer."

agrees with Rossouw, using concepts from narrative theory and technology to understand the reality of physicality: "storied bodies," "encoding our physical bodies," and "narratively constructed."[40]

Irrelevant of which perspective one might find more compelling, be it positive or negative, towards online worship, the conversation represents a larger phenomenon regarding the online reality, and that is polarization. In Jonathan Haidt's contemplation of social media since 2015, he proposed that the algorithmic enclaves and how news goes viral polarize Western society.[41]

If James Smith is correct in proposing that what we learn in the liturgy forms how we live, then online ritual breeds polarization.[42] But it is not a novum phenomenon in Christianity and not confined to online worship, but certainly even more when in virtual reality. It is interesting to note that research performed on three South African churches in the Charismatic tradition came to the following understanding of the way Holy Communion is practiced:

> Gathering from the responses from the respondents, it seems as though the atmosphere varies from church to church. It seems that everyone had a unique experience and that no real atmosphere is created for the members. As we understand it, everyone is left to create their own atmosphere and experience. This is clearly depicted in two of the churches where tables with the elements are made available and one can partake as one wishes.[43]

In these practices, the Holy Communion is quite frankly left to the impetus of the members. What transpires is not a counter-cultural formation of a human community but a strengthening of values that polarize human existence to the impetus of each individual. Or as Denny and Wepener opine: "The empirical-descriptive data presented in this article confirms that a culture of consumerism and individualism has clearly entered these worship services."[44]

Denny and Wepener go on to show that the Holy Communion is meant to be a moment of communal participation in the body of Christ as

---

40. Matthee, "Cyber Cemeteries," 218–20.
41. See Haidt, "Why the Past 10 Years."
42. Smith, *Desiring the Kingdom*, 17–18.
43. Denny and Wepener, "Spirit and the Meal," 6.
44. Denny and Wepener, "Spirit and the Meal," 7.

the fellowship of believers. Furthermore, as Desmond Tutu proposes, the community is fundamental to an African understanding of life:

> In Xhosa, we say, "Umntu ngumtu ngabantu." This expression is very difficult to render in English, but we could translate it by saying, "A person is a person through other persons." . . . For us, the solitary human being is a contradiction in terms. *Ubuntu* is the essence of being human. It speaks of how my humanity is caught up and bound up inextricably with yours. It says, not as Descartes did, "I think, therefore I am" but rather, "I am because I belong." I need other human beings in order to be human. The completely self-sufficient human being is subhuman. I can be me only if you are fully you. I am because we are, for we are made for togetherness, for family. We are made for complementarity. We are created for a delicate network of relationships, of interdependence with our fellow human beings, with the rest of creation.[45]

Building on Tutu's ubuntu as the interdependence of humans in relationship, I propose that the postcolonial Holy Communion should facilitate the formation of ubuntu in the sense of dislodging polarization towards cooperation, even when we do not agree completely with those we live with. The postcolonial liturgy should move towards decolonizing the mind, transforming public life towards a more inclusive and communal understanding of existing in this world.

Parody

> The reconciled and redeemed body of Christ is marked by cruciform practices that counter the liturgies of consumption, hoarding, and greed that characterize so much of our late modern culture. As a result, the ekklēsia is distinguished by very different procedures and criteria for the distribution of goods and wealth. In this sense, the church's mad economics anticipates a kingdom economics. . . . Sadly, in many contexts of worship in North America, the offering in worship is little more than a parody of such an alternative economics. —JAMES SMITH[46]

It is interesting to note the insistence of James Smith that the liturgy of the collection is supposed to counter the economic realities of consumption. At the same time, he laments that the collection has become merely a parody

---

45. Tutu, *God Is Not a Christian*, 21–22.
46. Smith, *Desiring the Kingdom*, 204–5.

POSTCOLONIAL LITURGICAL CONTEMPLATION

of its real purpose. From this perspective, the collection is supposed to be for those in need, as is evident in the appointment of the deacons in Acts 6 and the apostle Paul's collection for the needy in Jerusalem in 1 Cor 11.[47]

Not only is there a theologically unsophisticated dealing with the collection as a liturgical act, but with the wider economic system. Walter Mignolo is convinced that Christianity is in cahoots with the capitalist market democracy, which underscores the *parody* of the collection.[48] Ishmael Tetteh proposes that the system of commerce within Africa was laid there by the missional activity of colonial Christianity. At the same time, today, neoliberal capitalism is maintained by the Pentecostal and Charismatic Christian churches.[49]

Postcolonial thought, as counter, calls for "de-colonial epistemic shift[s]" which can imagine other ways of existing in the world, "other economy [sic], other politics, other ethics."[50] Thus, the collection as liturgical practice ought to speak of an imagination of other economies. Such a liturgical practice would call for the decolonization of the mind, opening new economic ways in which more imaginative economic cooperation could be reliable. Vuyani Vellem indicates that the mind's decolonization is a "reject[ion of] the finality of the West."[51] However, it should be expanded to include a rejection of all economic finalities for the individual and larger community. Thus, the collection should imagine new economic possibilities. Yes, the collection must be named for its immediate effect of charity for those who require current resources, but it must also be more.

This being said, we must beware of the implications of charity. David Bosch[52] and Allan Boesak[53] have adequately critiqued charity. After all, charity colonizes the minds of both the receiver of charity, making them reliant, and the giver of charity, creating a superiority complex that underscores ideas of paternalism. Thus, the collection must move beyond the booby trap of charity towards imaginative possibilities. This means that the collection resources should aid the vulnerable, the poor, and the excluded in such a way that other economies are built in which they can participate,

---

47. Meyers, *Missional Worship, Worshipful Mission*, 185.
48. Mignolo, "Delinking," 463–64.
49. Tetteh, *Inspired African Mystical Gospel*, 25.
50. Mignolo, "Delinking," 453.
51. Vellem, "Un-Thinking the West," 8.
52. Bosch, *Transforming Mission*, 286.
53. Boesak, *Tenderness of Conscience*, 200.

rather than the exclusive nature of economies of authoritarianism. In this line of thought, such an economy goes beyond (without excluding) the immediate needs of people towards systems, organizations, and movements that struggle for sustainable living and working conditions for the most vulnerable. The imagination of collection becomes a moment of imagining local resources as a force for change, not just in a temporal manner, but in a sustainable manner.[54] I want to propose that the understanding of the collection is but one form of parody in contemporary liturgy, and reconciliation, the forgiveness of sins, baptism, and communion follow similar trends.

MOVING THE CENTER OF LITURGICAL PRACTICE: A POSTCOLONIAL IDENTITY

> The basic question was: from what base did African peoples look at the world? Eurocentrism or Afrocentrism? The question was not that of mutual exclusion between Africa and Europe but the basis and the starting point of their interaction. . . . [K]nowing oneself and one's environment was the correct basis of absorbing the world; that there could never be only one center from which to view the world but that different people in the world had their culture and environment as the center. The relevant question was therefore one of how one center related to other centers. —Ngũgĩ wa Thiong'o[55]

At the 2019 Theological Day of the University of the Free State, the theme was *The Church and Violence against Women and Children*. The liturgy (compiled by Reverend Martin Laubscher) embodied anger and lament through the readings of Suzanne Vega's song *Luka* and Paulette Kelly's poem *I Got Flowers Today* performed by female students. This liturgy embodied and hybridized language in two ways. Firstly, a lingual agency of the oppressed. And secondly, a convergence of secular language in sacred space. I propose that both movements represent a movement of centers and speak of identity from a postcolonial perspective.

More traditional liturgical practices are confounded to the usage of scriptural texts. This is apparent in a quick overview of liturgical proposals

---

54. The history of the collection shows a close association with economic well-being for those excluded by the status quo. See Cilliers and Wepener, "Herinnering aan die Kinders"; Wepener, *Aan Tafel Met Jesus*.

55. Wa Thiong'o, *Moving the Centre*, 26–27.

within *Woord en Fees*[56] and in *The Worship Sourcebook*.[57] The point could be made that biblical sources are neither religious nor Western. However, the history of interpretation of the Bible in Africa is a spiritualization and Westernization of the biblical text.

Regarding the postcolonization of liturgy, I want to propose the lived experience of a postcolonial identity as the c/enter[58] of the liturgy; thus, the lived experience of a postcolonial identity as a critical interlocutor of the liturgy.

In the Spanish television show *Money Heist*, the protagonists sing an Italian resistance song called "Bella Ciao."[59] Irrelevant to the storyline of *Money Heist*, the following documentary showcases how this protest song became world-renowned to the point where refugees entering the European Union would sing "Bella Ciao" upon arrival.[60] To put it differently, those who find themselves vulnerable and disenfranchised associate strongly with this song. The song's origin can be traced back to the Italian Resistance of the partisans against the invasion of Nazi Germany. And the final strophe speaks about the death of the partisan in this resistance for freedom.

From the lived experience of postcolonial identity, incorporating songs that become essential to the lived experience of the disenfranchised could benefit postcolonial liturgical practices.

In Emmanuel Lartey's book, *Postcolonializing God*, he contemplates a liturgical practice that he deems postcolonial. What is interesting about the description of this postcolonial liturgy is that it is secular to its very being. Although there are fundamentally religious practices, the government of Ghana organized the liturgy in 2007.

---

56. *Woord en Fees* is a yearly compilation of liturgical recommendations and commentaries within the Dutch Reformed Church based on the liturgical year and Revised Common Lectionary.

57. See Orsmond et al., *Woord en Fees*; Steenwyk and Witvliet, *Worship Sourcebook*.

58. I borrow "c/enter" from Simone Drichel, "Time of Hybridity," 605, to indicate that the center should be decentered in itself. As I have indicated in chapter 2, the moving of the center for postcolonial thought does not place a new center as normative, but rather asks how different centers relate to one another (see Wa Thiong'o, *Moving the Centre*, 26–27). Thus, movement is towards a plurality of legitimate centers in relation and interaction with each other.

59. Pina, "Money Heist."

60. Alfaro and Lejarreta, "Money Heist."

Three things are of great interest in tracing the postcolonial aspects: the music, the inclusion of prayers from three religious traditions, and the involvement of descendants of both victims of slavery and collaborators of slavery.[61]

The hymn of welcoming in this space is Osibisa's "Welcome Home,"[62] which speaks of a longing for home and, in this context, returning home from the African diaspora. Two things stand out for me. One, the music is thoroughly secular and speaks to the lived experience of enslaved people during colonization. Two, the welcoming includes the collaborators of colonization. The welcoming becomes a joy for both those who were sold into slavery and those who collaborated with slavery. The joy lies in welcoming, being welcomed, and healing relationships.

The second crucial postcolonial practice of this liturgy lies in the prayers of invocation by religious leaders from three different religious traditions: Christian, Muslim, and African Traditional Religion.[63] This inclusion of interreligious prayers underscores the lived experience of a postcolonial identity who finds herself within the global community of religious pluralism. Furthermore, integrating other religious traditions opens the opportunity for empathic interaction in society through an "encounter with the religious other."[64] Furthermore, the pouring of libation was included as part and parcel of the prayers even though libation is mostly part of African Traditional Religious expression. Libation here underscores African spirituality whereby recognition of evil and good spiritual forces occurs. However, this recognition seeks blessing from the good forces.[65] In this sense, a postcolonial liturgy is contextually grounded and practiced in the likeness of the tradition of such a context.

The third postcolonial aspect of this liturgy is the cooperation between the descendants of Africans who were taken into slavery and the successors of traditional African rulers.[66] In representing the latter, Lartey showcases that the president declares and confesses guilt for participating in colonization and slavery. Hereafter, the traditional leaders step down from their positions of privilege to wash the hands of the diasporic Africans, adding

---

61. Lartey, *Postcolonializing God*, 38–64.
62. Lartey, *Postcolonializing God*, 47–48.
63. Lartey, *Postcolonializing God*, 49–50.
64. Cornille, "Empathy and Otherness," 221.
65. Lartey, *Postcolonializing God*, 49.
66. Lartey, *Postcolonializing God*, 51–53.

action to the confession.⁶⁷ It should be noted that traditional African rulers never do menial tasks in public settings. This liturgical action is thus a reversal of roles and, in essence, the possibility of identity fragmentation and fluidity.

In these three movements of a postcolonial liturgy, the three themes of postcolonial thought come to the fore. An unjust and totalitarian regime is undermined through new relationality. There is a movement from one central thought of truth to many possibilities of truth centers. And identity becomes hybrid and non-absolute.

From a South African and Afrikaans context, but in a similar manner, Cas Wepener proposed in his book *Kookpunt!*⁶⁸ the usage of angry poetry as liturgical practice.⁶⁹ Wepener is convinced that the South African lived experience is anger at contextual realities of injustice, poverty, corruption, police brutality, racism, poor leadership, and a lack of service delivery.⁷⁰ Once more, this lived experience is not restricted to a particular population group within South Africa:

> Poor people are angry, rich people are angry. Coloured people are angry, black people are angry, and white people are angry. Christians, Muslims, Hindus, and atheists are angry. It is a fact the people in South Africa have reached a boiling point or are at least quickly en route to reaching a boiling point. The examples are too many to name.⁷¹

Wepener proposes that Ingrid Jonker's poem, "Die Kind wat Geskiet Is Deur Soldate by Nyanga,"⁷² captures the spirit of anger in South Africa:

Wepener proposes that the child in the poem invites us to follow him in simultaneously meaningful anger and the lifting of our fists against oppression and corrupt powers in this world. Wepener showcases two crucial aspects of lived experience and the postcolonial liturgy. The first is an acute awareness of the contextual situation, both taking cognition thereof and

---

67. Lartey, *Postcolonializing God*, 52–53.
68. *Kookpunt!* was published in English as *Boiling Point!*
69. Wepener, *Kookpunt!*.
70. Wepener, *Kookpunt!*, 14–17.
71. Wepener, *Kookpunt!*, 16, my translation. Original text: "Arm mense is kwaad, ryk mense is kwaad. Christene, Moslems, Hindoes en ateïste is kwaad. Dat mense in Suid-Afrika kookpunt bereik het of ten minste vinnig op pad is daarheen, is 'n feit, en die voorbeelde is te veel om op te noem."
72. "The child who was shot by soldiers at Nyanga" (my translation).

moving towards working for a better future. The second is the incorporation of secular literature for the liturgy. Herein there is an awareness that liturgy is not without human and worldly experience. Liturgy is fundamentally conceived within life and named by the poets of our communities.

THE DISINTEGRATION AND POTENTIAL OF COMMUNITY

As I write this sentence, national and international lockdown measures are still in place regarding the COVID-19 pandemic. The loneliness and isolation that lockdown measures make more palpable are inherently human experiences, albeit partial and momentarily. Either way, these experiences could potentially speak of the disintegration of community, both with other human beings and God. Interestingly, Johan Cilliers has contemplated this as an empty communion table and proposed that the empty table does not indicate merely the lack of or disintegration of community but rather "a space of expectancy" where the presence of God, and by extension, of community could potentially come to the fore in the future.[73] The postcolonial liturgy understands this potential space of expectancy both in its potential to bring forth a more significant presence and community and the danger of relentless absence and everything in between.

As a case in point, Cas Wepener researched African Independent Churches on ritual to determine how bridging and linking capital worked regarding well-being.[74] What he found was inherently ambivalent; indeed, the rituals could potentially be a funnel toward communal cooperation toward social capital of well-being. However, the "strongest message is probably that bridging and linking capital are to a large extent absent in this community."[75] This is not the only perspective, though. The work of Joel Cabrita showcases that an African Independent Church, the Church of the Nazaretha, formed identity, agency, and creativity through alternative forms of writing and religious education in their struggle for survival in the apartheid context:

> Apartheid-era African agents read and created texts in ways that reinvented, shifted, and distorted the official bureaucratic

---

73. Cilliers, *Dancing with Deity*, 189–10.
74. Wepener, "Eating and Drinking."
75. Wepener, "Eating and Drinking," 176–77.

repertoire. Johannes Shembe's creation of an ecclesial bureaucracy offers a rich example of one such imaginative appropriation of a seemingly hegemonic official documentary culture.[76]

Cabrita's point is that this usage of texts, and the close association with an oral tradition, functioned to "knit [the] congregation together into intimate, face-to-face communities."[77] Inherently the perspective, and the point one wants to make, would influence the relationality between the ritual and the actual implication of the ritual. For postcolonial liturgical contemplation, the point is not in the outcomes per se but rather the potential of liturgy to both bring forth good and evil, in essence, the fluid and ambivalent nature of the liturgy itself to create identity.

I would argue that the disruption of COVID-19 merely unveils human vulnerability and the potential for danger and woundedness. In this sense, all of the human experience is inherently decentered. No one is without either agency or creativity. No one is a complete stranger or thorough acquaintance. No one is central or perifery. No one is powerful or powerless. No one is completely good or evil. Instead, we are all in some of these conditions, and at different times, any combination. I would propose that in acknowledging our variety of potential combinations and disparities of identity, we find ourselves more alike to those around us, just as decentered in their identity as ourselves, and the community is reorientated towards the potential for renewed relationality.

THE SOUTH AFRICAN MYTH OF GOVERNMENTAL PATERNITY

South Africa's history includes colonization and that particular type of colonization called apartheid. I have engaged these realities. However, postcolonial thought transpires merely the colonial reality of the past, proposing the possibility that new myths can and will become tyrannical in the present, inevitably acting just like colonization, even as it has been rebranded. This is the realization that there is no instant liberation from human corruption and that any liberation is a constant struggle.

Today's South African context has brought forth a fascinating neocolonial myth in the form of governmental paternity that claims to be in

---

76. Cabrita, "Texts, Authority, and Community," 63.
77. Cabrita, "Texts, Authority, and Community," 73.

the liberation traditions against colonialism. It is true that the African National Congress (ANC), which governs South Africa, has historically been a liberation movement, but when it encourages participation in the #BlackLivesMatter movement as if South African police brutality is also in our context that of racist white men, then one cannot but agree with Herman Mashaba as he notes:

> Why are South Africans being called upon by our government to support a movement on the other side of the world, when this same government of ours has killed poor black people with callous disregard for decades?[78]

Mashaba goes on to name what is happening in South Africa through this very government's acts; the denial of HIV/AIDS existence, the killing of Andries Tatane in 2011, the Marikana Massacre on August 16, 2012, leaving 34 mineworkers dead and 78 injured (our current president was on the board of the Lonmin mine where the incident took place at the time of the massacre), the death of 143 vulnerable patients in 2014, and 11 deaths at the hands of law enforcement during the COVID-19 lockdown. Poor black people in South Africa cannot breathe. But it is a more painful breathlessness, magnified by the myth that this government cares about liberation and freedom for the previously oppressed.[79]

Even more, the South African Institute of Race Relations has proposed that racism is not nearly as prevalent as claimed by political leaders and that the ANC uses racism as a scapegoat for their own incompetencies in creating an adequate economic and social context.[80]

During COVID-19, the South African government followed strict lockdown measures, similar to Developed Countries, regardless of contextual differences. Research six months into the lockdown measures has proposed that as much as "a decade's worth of jobs [were lost] in less than half a year of lockdown and the economy slowed by 16.4%."[81] As South Africa is a country with a massive percentage of joblessness which the government cannot rectify or soften with its lousy stipend of R350 (about $19) per month, the potential loss of well-being for these measures may well outweigh the gains.

78. Mashaba, "Black Lives Need to Matter," para 4.
79. Mashaba, "Black Lives Need to Matter," para 4.
80. Jeffery, "Critical Race Theory," 8.
81. Finfind, "SA SMME COVID-19 Impact Report," 1.

Postcolonial Liturgical Contemplation

On February 9, 2023, the ANC announced a state of disaster because of the ongoing energy crisis in South Africa. According to BusinessTech, the state of disaster allows the government to accelerate change in the affairs of energy production without due diligence from civil society, although the energy sector has always been a state monopoly.[82] This has brought forth pushback on the point that the government has inherently created the crisis for a state of disaster through mismanagement, corruption, and dysfunction.

Achille Mbembe has showcased that this myth of paternal authority is by no means a novel phenomenon on the African continent after liberation. In Cameroon, the ruling party would propagate itself similarly as the figure and keeper of all things good for society, as if it is society itself, with the proposal that citizens should merely follow its authority to the tee.[83] Mbembe describes the spectacle of this situation as the insistence by the government for loyalty. However, from the citizens' side, there would be a linguistic and mimetic revolt, reconfiguring linguistic loyalty so that it plays the fool with the government.[84] For instance, "metaphors meant to glorify state power; with a simple tonal shift, one metaphor could take on many meanings."[85]

This playful revolt comes naturally to the secular rituals within the context of the myth of state paternity and sole authority. It furthermore represents the decolonial impetus of struggle against forces that halter or disrupt the agency of the citizenry. During the South African lockdown, one specific enforcement of a law that seemed ridiculous in its explanation invoked comedic mimetic resistance. It regarded a complete restriction on the usage of tobacco products. In the words of the health minister, Nkosazana Dlamini-Zuma:

> When people zol,[86] they put saliva on the paper, and then zol, and then they share that zol. . . . But also, they are moving saliva from one to the other.[87]

---

82. Staff Writer, "State of Disaster."
83. Mbembe, *On the Postcolony*, 105.
84. Mbembe, *On the Postcolony*, 105–6.
85. Mbembe, *On the Postcolony*, 106.
86. Zol is South African slang for a rolled cannabis joint, but meant in this context to refer to a rolled cigarette.
87. Nkosazana Dlamini-Zuma, from Newzroom Afrika, "No Alcohol and Tobacco Sales," 2:32–2:54. See also Pitjeng, "'When People Zol,'" para. 5.

This direct recording of her words was transformed into a song by Max Hurrel[88] and a music video by The Kiffness.[89] What transpired from there was a myriad of TikTok videos in which South Africans choreographed dance moves mimicking her words towards satire and mockery.[90] One could claim that this ritual was merely entertainment for the lockdown period. And yet, therein lies the possibility of an implicit pushback against governmental paternity that is illogical to local existence. In the words of Homi Bhabha, "mimicry emerges as the representation of a difference that is itself a process of disavowal."[91]

The postcolonial liturgy would do well to take note of mimicry and secular ritual for praxis.

LITURGICAL FORMATION AS C/ENTER SPACE FOR THE DECOLONIAL CONSCIOUSNESS

In James Smith's book, *Desiring the Kingdom*, he describes the Christian liturgy as the present time, which hopes for the future and remembers the past. Borrowing from Charles Taylor, he uses the phrase "higher times" to describe the culmination of the past, present, and future in the liturgy of the church.[92] At the same time, this description opposes what he calls "CNN-ized time" which is "an orientation to what's coming that lacks hope; instead, it simply records the onslaught of events."[93]

Building upon this understanding, he moves to the congregation as those who are called in the present time to participate in worship both as remembrance and hope.[94] This understanding of worship brings the possibility of acute honesty as "our current not-yet gatherings [that] will have to constantly confess their failures."[95] Framed from a postcolonial perspective, there is the potential formation of a people who have an honest awareness of a colonial past that transcends into our present times. When Smith

---

88. See Max Hurrell's parody song "ZOL," created in 2020.
89. The Kiffness, "Max Hurrell."
90. TikTok Africa Official, "ZOL Challenge TikTok."
91. Bhabha, *Location of Culture*, 86.
92. Smith, *Desiring the Kingdom*, 158.
93. Smith, *Desiring the Kingdom*, 159.
94. Smith, *Desiring the Kingdom*, 159–61.
95. Smith, *Desiring the Kingdom*, 161.

contemplates the potential of the future as the community's vocation, he frames it as a call to be human:

> We are commissioned as God's image bearers, his vice-regents, charged with the task of "ruling" and caring for creation . . . unfolding and unfurling its latent possibilities through human making—in short, through *culture*.[96]

As far as I can discern, this idea is quite profound in a South African context which has often been at odds with culture through the colonial project. At the same time, in a multicultural space, one must add the importance of the latent potential of cultures, not culture in the singular. What precisely would the implications for "human making" be where these cultures intersect and dissent is open for discussion; but this would indeed open a space of negotiation and contention, which the postcolonial liturgy must allow.

Smith goes on to show it is about being called to bring one's culture to the liturgy and forming culture through the liturgy.[97] There is thus a double movement of cultural influence on the liturgy and liturgical influence on culture.[98] I am convinced, however, that this movement from culture to liturgy to culture cannot be understood epistemologically as two completely different worlds. The liturgical influence on culture may bring with it a formation of Christians, but that does not mean this formation goes radically outside and beyond the system of thought of the culture. In other words, the potential cultural novelties through the decolonization of consciousness and a postcolonial identity bring forth other ways of thinking, imagining, and dreaming in liturgical formation beyond what the past has bestowed on us.

Therefore, the postcolonial liturgy anticipates faith formation as the c/entering of the decolonial consciousness. Two movements are meant here, that the decolonial consciousness is c/entral, with the noticeable realization that the slash (/) indicates the myriad of centers involved and thus a simultaneous decentering in the centering. And secondly, the possibility exists, within its potential for success and failure, of a new culture entering the liturgical space and the consequent faith formation.

---

96. Smith, *Desiring the Kingdom*, 163.

97. Smith, *Desiring the Kingdom*, 164.

98. See also Lutheran World Federation, "Chicago Statement on Worship and Culture"; Lutheran World Federation's Study Team on Worship and Culture, "Nairobi Statement."

Postcolonial Homiletics?
An Attempt at a Postcolonial Liturgy

GATHERING[99]

† Call to Worship:

Liturgist (L):   Praise the Lord, all you nations. Extol him, all you peoples.

Faith Community (C): For great is his love toward us, and the faithfulness of the Lord endures forever.

L: The Lord has done great things for us, and we are filled with joy.

C: In our suffering and struggle; in our poverty and sorrow; in our homelessness and hunger; in our flight from danger: The Lord has done great things for us.

L: Those who sow with tears will reap with songs of joy. Praise the Lord![100]

† Welcoming:

L: Whether we are old or young,
whether we are first-time or long-time worshippers,
whether we come full of doubts or confidence, joy or sorrow,
whether we are privileged or not, struggling or thriving.
In this place, we are all family.
Along with the church in every nation around the world.
Although we may be different in race, class, culture, and language,
In Jesus Christ, we are united.
Welcome to all of you today.
The Lord be with you![101]

† Prayer of Adoration:

L: Father-Mother God, present in all things as the substance of existence; you embody the entire universe in material, energy, law, and cohesive love.

---

99. In this liturgy I will be following the five movements proposed in *The Worship Sourcebook*: Gathering, Proclamation, Response to the Word, The Lord's Supper, and Sending. Steenwyk and Witvliet, *Worship Sourcebook*, 25.

100. Based on Ps 117 and Ps 126, NIV.

101. Based on Steenwyk and Witvliet, *Worship Sourcebook*, 60.

C: **You formed us, love us, and sustain us in all we need.**

L: Mother-Father God, all things find their existence in you, and you are the only power, wisdom, and presence.

C: **You have given us the privilege of participating in your very existence as community.**

L: In your presence, we are because you are.

C: **And together, we exist with each other and for each other, to wield power and wisdom for the benefit and well-being of all our brothers and sisters.**

L: Great-Father Great-Mother God, for your gracious love for us, we praise you.

C: **Amen.**[102]

† Confession:

L: The painful injustices of the past still haunt us today. We are the children of the colonizers and colonized, the slave traders and chiefs who sold their people, the architects of apartheid, and those who did not speak out.

C: **Lord, have mercy.**

L: We are a people who, even today, live in the shadows of injustice. We often fail to name evil, to do the good we can do, and to uphold the hopes of our democracy.

C: **Christ, have mercy.**

L: Lord, you have commissioned us to love one another as we love ourselves; to search for righteousness; to bring about the good news of your salvation and love for the whole cosmos; and to care for the vulnerable, the poor, the marginalized, and the stranger. So often, we have failed.

C: **Lord, have mercy.**

† Assurance of Pardon:

---

102. Based on Tetteh, *Fountain of Life*; Tutu, *God Is Not a Christian*, 21–22.

L: Community of the Lord, hear the good news. Although we have erred in our ways; although our minds have been colonized by the powers of the past and present; we can be assured that there is another King whose kingdom is that of justice and righteousness; a kingdom where those who work will have their fill and peace will exist not merely in political slogans. Through this King, our Lord Jesus Christ, freedom is proclaimed to you. He refreshes our souls and leads us on the right paths.[103]

† The Law:

L: We respond to God's pardon of debts by pursuing a consciousness that envisions human life as rich with possibilities of thinking, understanding, relating, sharing, and living with one another.

C: **God's command lies not in any one correct way of existing but in how we relate to one another.**

L: Thus, our Lord Jesus Christ has said: "A new commandment I give to you, that you love one another just as I have loved you."[104]

† Song of Dedication:

A song to be sung which represents the locality and experience of the underside of society.

† Service of Baptism:[105]

Words of Institution

L: Community of faith, through Christ's work of reconciliation, we have reconciled with God and one another. This reconciliation means a unity that binds us together in the Spirit of the Lord. No more is there a place for separation, enmity, and hatred between people, either physically or mentally. The only condition for membership in the

---

103. Based on Isa 65:21–25; Acts 13:39; Ps 23:3, NIV.
104. Based on Wa Thiong'o, *Moving the Centre*, 26; John 13:34, NRSV.
105. Based on "Confession of Belhar"; Steenwyk and Witvliet, *Worship Sourcebook*, 260–88.

community of faith is true faith in Jesus Christ. And so, we welcome [*Name(s)*] as part of this community through the initiation of baptism.

Presentation—For the Baptism of Infants

L: In presenting your child for baptism, you announce your faith in Jesus Christ.
We/I do.

Presentation—For the Baptism of Adults or Older Children

L: In having heard God's promise and commission, do you desire to be baptized?
I do.

Profession of Faith

L: Do you believe that God's Spirit has given us the gift and obligation of unity and that this community is the church for, with, and of all humanity?
We/I do.

L: Do you believe that Christ has brought reconciliation between God and humanity and that we are called to participate in this reconciliation?
We/I do.

L: Do you believe that God has revealed himself as the one who wished justice and peace among people and that this community is called to struggle for justice and peace?
We/I do.

Prayer of Thanksgiving

L: Mother-Father, God of the destitute, the poor, and the wronged. You free the prisoner and restore sight to the blind. You support the oppressed, protect the stranger, help orphans and widows, and block the ways of the wicked. We thank you, Father-Mother of all, for welcoming us into your very being; for standing with us when we were wronged, impoverished, and miserable; for reconciling ourselves with you, uniting us with each other, and wishing justice and peace for us in your ongoing work in the world through your Son, Jesus Christ, and the Holy Spirit. May this moment of participation in baptism be a witness to our involvement in reconciliation and unity, and may your Holy Spirit fill our hearts and minds with a renewed commitment to justice and peace for all of humanity. Jesus is Lord. To the one and only God, Parent, Son, and Holy Spirit, be the honor and glory for ever and ever. **Amen.**

Baptism

L: [*Name*], you are baptized in the name of the Father-Mother, and of the Son, and of the Holy Spirit. **Amen.**

Blessing

L: [*Name*], in baptism, you have become part of the one holy, universal Christian church, the communion of saints called from the entire human family. **Amen.**

Welcoming

L: Sisters and brothers, we receive [name(s)] into Christ's church today. Do you welcome [*them*] in love, and do you promise to pray for, encourage, and help nurture [*them*] in the faith?

C: We do, God helping us.

Intercessory Prayer

L: Gracious God and Mother of all. We thank you for gathering, protecting, and caring for this faith community and your church throughout the world, in every nation, of every culture, and through every language. We pray for [*name(s)*]. Bless and strengthen [*them*] daily as active agents of your unity, reconciliation, and justice in this world. Uphold [*them*] through your Spirit. Unfold to [*them*] your love and grace. Deepen [*their*] faith. Keep [*them*] from the power of evil. And enable [*them*] to live a holy and blameless life until your kingdom comes. **Amen.**

PROCLAMATION

Postcolonial Liturgical Contemplation

† Prayer for Illumination:

L: Lord God, our Father and Mother, protector of the innocent and vulnerable and strength for the weak; by your Holy Spirit and Word, lead our minds from slavery to liberation and open our thoughts to your will. Through Jesus Christ, we pray. **Amen.**

RESPONSE TO THE WORD

† Prayers of the People:[106]

L: Our Parent in heaven, in the place of power over the universe.

C: **Our loyalty belongs to you alone and not to any earthly power.**

L: Hallowed be your name in your community of faith's conscious remembrance of what you have done for all humanity.

C: **You have liberated us from all forms of oppression towards a life of peace amongst each other.**

L: Let your kingdom come into our minds and imaginations through other ways of relating, existing, and living in this world.

C: **And your will be done, on earth as it is in heaven.**

L: Give them and us today our daily bread. May we have enough to live with well-being in this world, but not more than we need.

C: **May we never be begging people, nor greedy people.**

L: Forgive us our debts, as we have forgiven our debtors.

C: **Fathom in us an understanding of a more just economic way of relating to our sisters and brothers from every sphere and position of life.**

L: And lead us not into the temptation of abusing power, negating other ways of perceiving and understanding the world, and being quiet about injustice.

C: **But deliver us from the evil inside ourselves, which works against the well-being of all of humanity and creation.**

L: For yours is the kingdom, power, and glory forever.

Amen.

---

106. Based on the Lord's Prayer, Matt 6:9–13, NIV.

† Invitation to the Offering:

L: The earth is the Lord's, and everything in it, the world, and all who live in it. When Israel was given the Promised Land, they were told that there need not be any poor people amongst them, for the Lord had blessed them in abundance. However, provision has been made for the unequal distribution of God's abundance through tithing. A tenth of all produce was to be set aside for the foreigner, the orphan, the widow, and all the vulnerable who do not have enough to live. Let justice flow like a river and righteousness like a never-failing stream![107]

† Offering Prayer:[108]

L: Blessed are you, God of all creation; we have these gifts to share through your goodness. Accept and use our offerings for your glory and your kingdom's service.

C: Blessed be God forever. Amen.

THE LORD'S SUPPER

† Declaration of God's Invitation and Promises:

L: Jesus said: "Come to me, all you who are weary and burdened, and I will give you rest."[109]

C: Here at this table, we all come from our places of suffering and struggle, from poverty and uncertainty, from weariness and a hope for the future.

L: People will come from east, west, and north and south and will take their places at the feast in the kingdom of God.[110]

C: Not just some are welcome at the table. Not one culture, or language, or class, or race, or gender, or sexual orientation, or any other characteristic defines our worthiness to be at this table.

L: All are invited and welcome just as you come.

---

107. Based on Ps 24:1; Deut 15:4; 26:12; and Amos 5:24, NIV.
108. Steenwyk and Witvliet, *Worship Sourcebook*, 240.
109. Matt 11:28, NIV.
110. Based on Luke 13:29, NIV.

Postcolonial Liturgical Contemplation

† Great Prayer of Thanksgiving:

L: It is truly good for us to glorify you, Mother-Father, and to thank you. You alone are God, the living and beautiful one, dwelling in the place of absolute power over all of creation from before time and forever. You are the fountain of all life and the source of all existence. You made all things and filled them with your blessing. You created them to rejoice in the splendor of your very being.[111]

C: **Lord, you are the greatest artist.**
To whom no one can compare,
Streaking sunsets very beautiful,
Painting rainbows in the air.

L: Almighty God, Parent of all, you loved the world so much that you sent your only Son to be our Saviour in the fullness of time. Incarnate by the Holy Spirit, born of the Virgin Mary, he lived as one of us yet was without sin. To the poor, he proclaimed the good news of salvation; to prisoners, freedom; to the sorrowful, joy. To fulfill your purpose, he gave himself up to death and, rising from the grave, destroyed death and made the whole creation new.[112]

C: **Christ has died,**
Christ has risen,
Christ will come again.

L: Almighty Father-Mother, we thank you for your Holy Spirit, your first gift to all who are part of the faith community. You have given us and your church everywhere your Spirit to participate in your work of reconciliation, unity, and justice in the world and to bring to fulfillment the sanctification of all.[113]

C: **May your Spirit lead us on these paths of righteousness to the honor of your name.**

L: Lord, you have given us this meal of remembrance and liberation. You have called us to eat and remember your body as particular liberation for us all. May we so also be reminded of other bodies; the bodies of

---

111. Based on Steenwyk and Witvliet, *Worship Sourcebook*, 318.
112. Steenwyk and Witvliet, *Worship Sourcebook*, 320.
113. Based on Steenwyk and Witvliet, *Worship Sourcebook*, 321.

the poor who suffer in the cold, the bodies of women who are vulnerable to abuse, the bodies of the disabled who are often excluded, and the bodies of men broken by unjust economies. May we see your body in our neighbor's body and your face in the face of the vulnerable.

C: **Through your body, we are a new family, not of race or bloodline, but the family of God.**

L: You have called us to drink this cup of covenant sealed in your blood, which is for the forgiveness of sins. Your forgiveness of our debts makes all human divisions null and void. All human judgment is suspended, and all inferiority or superiority complexes are made invalid.

C: **May we be reminded at this table that you included the excluded and welcomed the other. Amen.**

† Passing of the Peace:

L: Thanks be to God: Christ makes us one. The peace of Christ be with you all.

As part of our call to reconciliation, unity, and justice, we have been commissioned to make peace with one another. Jesus has taught us to reconcile with those who may have something against us before we gather in worship. Thus, before we gather at the table, let's take this opportunity to greet each other with the words: "Peace to you."

The faith community greets each other with the passing of the peace and gathers around the table in a circle.

† Preparing the Bread and the Cup[114]

L: [*Breaking the one loaf of bread*] The bread that we break is a sharing in the body of Christ.

C: **We who are many are one body, for we all share the same loaf.**

L: [*Pouring the cup*] The cup for which we give thanks is a sharing in the blood of Christ.

C: **The cup that we drink is our participation in the blood of Christ.**

† Communion:

---

114. Steenwyk and Witvliet, *Worship Sourcebook*, 309.

Postcolonial Liturgical Contemplation

Invitation

L: Hear the words of our Lord: "Come to me, all you who are weary and burdened, and I will give you rest. Take my yoke upon you and learn from me, for I am gentle and humble in heart, and you will find rest for your souls. For my yoke is easy and my burden is light."[115]

All is ready at this table. Come and be welcomed.

C: **We come not because we must but because we have been invited. We come not because we are holy but because we have received grace. We come not because we are powerful but because God is with us in our weakness. We come not because we are pure but because we are welcome even in the fragmentation of our diverse identities.**[116]

Distribution

As the bread and cup are shared with one another.

C: **The body of Christ, given for you.**

The blood of Christ, shed for you.

† Response of Thanksgiving:

L: Lord God, our Parent, our Mother, our Father, our Sustainer, our Caregiver, in gratitude and joy for this moment of participation at your Table, with these people and your church all over the world, we give all we are to you. Lead us to live in this world as participants in your mission of reconciliation and justice. We have shared the living bread; we cannot leave unchanged. Ask much of us, expect much from us, enable much by us, and encourage many through us. So, Lord, may we live in ways that glorify you, as people of this earth and these earthly kingdoms, yet as citizens of the kingdom of heaven. **Amen.**[117]

SENDING

† Call to Service:

L: Go into the world: dance, laugh, sing, and create.

C: **We go with the assurance of God's blessing.**

---

115. Matt 11:28–29, NIV.
116. Based on Steenwyk and Witvliet, *Worship Sourcebook*, 342.
117. Based on Steenwyk and Witvliet, *Worship Sourcebook*, 345–46.

L: Go into the world: risk, explore, discover, and love.

C: We go with the assurance of God's grace.

L: Go into the world: believe, hope, struggle, and remember.

C: We go with the assurance of God's love. Thanks be to God![118]

† Blessing:

L: The grace of our Lord Jesus Christ be with you all.[119]

C: Amen.

---

118. Steenwyk and Witvliet, *Worship Sourcebook*, 354.
119. 2 Thess 3:18, NIV.

Chapter 4

Contemplating Postcolonial Hermeneutics

I HAVE DISCUSSED POSTCOLONIAL thought for homiletics and liturgy in this book. However, the homiletic endeavor should not be considered adequate without contemplating hermeneutics. After all, to preach is to interpret the biblical text within the broader socioeconomic and political context of our positionality. Thus, this chapter will contemplate postcolonial hermeneutics for postcolonial preaching.

HERMENEUTICS AND THE DECOLONIZATION OF THE MIND

> Decolonization of knowledge shall be understood in the constant double movement of unveiling the geo-political location of theology, secular philosophy and scientific reason and simultaneously affirming the modes and principles of knowledge that have been denied by the rhetoric of Christianization, civilization, progress, development, market democracy. —WALTER MIGNOLO[1]

The double movement of the decolonization of the mind certainly questions the reception of Christian interpretation of the biblical text. Let us consider that Mignolo is correct in the proposal that the Western interpretation of the biblical text is historically equal to all things colonial. Two viable options: get rid of this colonial text or reinterpret it. The first is possible, but I am not interested in such a direction.

---

1. Mignolo, "Delinking," 463.

Naming the Irrational Myth(s) within the Interpretation History of the Biblical Text

> Under postcolonial theory, theologians argue that biblical texts have been marked as powerful rhetorical instruments of imperialism. But at the same time, biblical texts have also been proclaimed in colonial settings and therefore contain a voice of justice that energizes faith to challenge injustice committed against the weak.
> —Lazare Rukundwa[2]

As is evident in the quote by Lazare Rukundwa, the naming of the irrational myth(s) within the biblical text itself has already enjoyed the privilege of being taken seriously. In conversation with many African thinkers, Rukundwa deconstructs Western hermeneutics as "foreign hermeneutics [which] are incapable of explaining the harsh realities of inequality, oppression, and exploitation often experienced in tricontinental countries."[3] To be clear, Rukundwa understands the Bible as "a cultural product in time and space" where the questions of authority should be directed not to the Bible itself but to "the authority of biblical interpretation." Similarly, Rasiah Sugirtharajah shows that one of the activities of postcolonial criticism is the "rereading and reinterpreting [of literary productions], and exposing the revisions or reinforcements of colonial or national history."[4]

Considering these proposals, we must determine whether it is the case that biblical interpretation has historically indeed been influenced by colonial sentiments. As a case in point, let us consider the commentary of F.W. Grosheide on Acts 10, published in 1941.

Two aspects of Grosheide's commentary are of importance. Firstly, he strongly proposes that this text underscores the new reality in Christ that God makes no distinction between people. In Grosheide's words: "Petrus stelt vast, dat God geen aannemer des persoons is."[5] However, and this is the second important aspect of his interpretation, irrelevant to God's lack of distinction, Grosheide underscores the gatekeeping persona of Peter. He claims that Acts 10 is inherently about the "bijzondere taak der apostelen"[6]

---

2. Rukundwa, "Postcolonial Theory," 340.

3. Rukundwa, "Postcolonial Theory," 344.

4. Sugirtharajah, *Exploring Postcolonial Biblical Criticism*, 14.

5. Grosheide, *Handelingen der Apostelen*, 168. "Peter determines that God is not an endorser of persons" (my translation).

6. "Special task of the apostles" (my translation).

Contemplating Postcolonial Hermeneutics

to preach the gospel to the gentiles.[7] The implication is that Cornelius' inclusion into the faith depends on this preaching. Grosheide proposes an interesting interpretation of verse 44, where Peter is interrupted by the Holy Spirit falling on these gentiles. He merely claims that Peter had said everything which needed to be said and that nothing more needed to be said. He asks rhetorically: "wat had Petrus nog meer moeten prediken in deze omstandigheden?"[8]

In this line of thinking, Grosheide's interpretation of Acts 10 and his focus on the gatekeeping persona of the apostle can be interpreted as a representation of a Westernized epistemology of Christianity. Thus, Grosheide proposes that faith needs the preaching of authority to establish the gospel. Although his interpretation includes the concept that God makes no distinction between people, the relaying of faith is impossible without the authority of the persona of the apostle. This paradigm of authority fits closely into paradigms of inclusion and exclusion proposed by historical interpretation of ecclesia. As David Bosch proposes:

> [The Protestant] mentality often hardly differed from that of Rome; where the Catholic model insisted on "outside the *church* no salvation," the Protestant model adhered to "outside the *word*, no salvation" (Knitter 1985:135). In both these models, mission essentially meant conquest and displacement. Christianity was understood to be unique, exclusive, superior, definitive, normative, and absolute (cf Knitter 1985:18), the only religion which had the divine right to exist and extend itself.[9]

It would not be far-fetched to take Grosheide's proposal and preach a sermon claiming that, although God makes no distinction between people, non-Christians should receive the gospel through the sanctioned church traditions or biblical interpretation. Such a sermon may go as far as to propose an adherence to the Western ecclesial and, per implication, Western cultural ways.

Thus, in an attempt to name the irrational myth(s) in the interpretation history of Acts 10, one could question how Peter, as the bearer of normativity, is understood. The fact that Cornelius was the one who initiated the meeting might indicate a reversal of roles. Or when the Holy Spirit

---

7. Grosheide, *Handelingen der Apostelen*, 169.

8. Grosheide, *Handelingen der Apostelen*, 171. "What more should Peter have been preaching in these circumstances?" (my translation).

9. Bosch, *Transforming Mission*, 491, original italics.

interrupts Peter, this may suggest that God silences Peter, as if he should listen rather than speak. Grosheide also ignores that Peter is staying at the house of Simon, the tanner.[10] Simon, the tanner, would have been considered unclean in Jewish understanding as his occupation expected him to work with dead flesh.[11] Thus, Peter's normative center may be questionable from the very onset. Furthermore, the myth that the Christian faith comes from normative and Western authority could thus be deconstructed, and new possibilities opened.

Decolonization of the Mind and Alternative Interpretation(s)

> However, if in the framing of postcolonial hermeneutics it is in the final instance not concerned with the "truth of the text" but rather with the central issue of the texts' promotion of colonial ideology (Sugirtharajah 1998a:19), its usefulness on the African continent where the Bible is still highly valued for many reasons, becomes a concern. If the Bible is studied only for identifying "those intrinsic textual features which embody colonial codes," and when the value of studying these texts for their own sakes or for theological and spiritual inspiration are secondary at best, it remains a question whether postcolonial hermeneutics are not short-circuiting itself, in Africa, but also elsewhere. —Jeremy Punt[12]

Punt correctly showcases a tendency in postcolonial thought to deconstruct biblical interpretation as merely colonial. As an antidote, an adequate postcolonial hermeneutic ought to construct alternative interpretations of the biblical text, and as I have showcased, in the vision of decolonizing the mind. As Rasiah Sugirtharajah proposes, one possibility is "[t]ransgressing the contrastive way of thinking."[13] The hermeneutic method here would be to question dualistic thinking, which is so prevalent in the colonial mythos, proposing instead that there are overlapping and intersectional similarities between colonizer/colonist, center/margin, religious/atheist, etc. Lis Valle calls this idea "a worldview of 'complementary dualities.'"[14] A similar idea is prevalent in Aimé Césaire's thought on how colonization is detrimental

---

10. Acts 9:42, NIV.
11. See Jennings, *Acts*, 101.
12. Punt, "Postcolonial Biblical Criticism," 71–72.
13. Sugirtharajah, *Exploring Postcolonial Biblical Criticism*, 15.
14. Valle, "Toward Postcolonial Liturgical Preaching," 28.

to both the colonized and the colonizer.[15] Thus, the identities and lived experiences of supposed opposites overlap and intersect. Valle goes even further, proposing that opposites need each other, complement each other, and are intertwined in identity formation.[16]

Returning to Acts 10, the interpretation of Willie Jennings transgresses the dualities laid by the colonial mythos in two locations. Firstly, the site of the relationship between Jew and gentile:

> God has pushed [Peter] over the line that separated Jewish bodies from Gentile bodies, holy bodies from unholy ones and pressed Peter to change his speech acts by never again calling anyone unholy or unclean.[17]

Unlike the immense commitment the colonial mythos has shown for assigning and maintaining separation, hierarchy, and authority, Jennings indicates that God's action in this text eradicates such separation. Furthermore, for Jennings, the speech act within the text overlaps and intersects. Even more, it breaks with the idea that the gospel comes from the apostle to the gentiles. Not only is Peter's speech act changed in the transgression of boundaries, but "Peter listens and hears the word of God in new and unanticipated places," and only then does he speak his truth.[18] Jennings makes the point that, from the outset of the meeting between Peter and Cornelius, the gospel first comes to Peter. Cornelius is the first to speak, and Peter listens to new possibilities of God's work. Jennings continues:

> Listening for the word of God in others who are not imagined with God, not imagined as involved with God, but whom God has sought out and is bringing near to the divine life and to our lives.[19]

Only then Peter speaks. Only then Peter realizes ultimately that his speaking can no longer be found in the dualities of holy/unholy, clean/unclean, or Jew/gentile. He deeply realizes, only at this moment, that "God does not show favoritism."[20]

---

15. Césaire, *Discourse on Colonialism*, 41.
16. Valle, "Toward Postcolonial Liturgical Preaching," 30.
17. Jennings, *Acts*, 110.
18. Jennings, *Acts*, 111.
19. Jennings, *Acts*, 111.
20. Acts 10:34, NIV.

But even this is not the end of the reversal, and Peter is not the last to speak. At the end of his sermon, Peter is interrupted by the Holy Spirit, and those with him are "astonished" that the gentiles are now speaking in tongues.[21] According to Jennings, and I quote,

> Nothing prepared them for this witness. Nothing suggested that this was coming. They certainly imagined their witness to the world of the diaspora, maybe even to a world beyond that diaspora, but never a witness *from the Gentiles to them*. The Gentiles speak in tongues, and Israel hears.[22]

This is the par excellence transgressing of the dualities of the colonial mythos and proposing another way of interpreting the text toward decolonizing the mind. Roles are reversed, and the activity of God comes not from the authoritative location of the apostle but from the unexpected action of the Holy Spirit through the mouths of the gentiles. It is interesting to take note of Virginia Burrus' understanding of heteroglossia within Luke-Acts. Using Mikhail Bakhtin's theory of heteroglossia as "polyglot consciousness," Burrus proposes that speaking in tongues represents alienation and denaturalization of speech.[23] In the context of Acts 10, the polyglot consciousness represents the decentralization of authority from whence God's revelation may, can, and does come.

The second transgression of the colonial mythos within Jennings' thought is found in the person of God. Jennings claims that Acts 10 is about "divine transgression."[24] It is God who, against the Old Testament laws, longs for the integration of bodies and refuses the separation of bodies. When Jennings makes this point, the identity of God is decolonized from the colonial Christian understanding that salvation is brought through a closed systematic theology where God cannot change and has already preordained the world within the dualities of the colonial worldview. According to postcolonial thinkers, this worldview was instrumental in underscoring colonial oppressions, such as racism, apartheid, and the eradication of alternative knowledge systems.[25]

21. Acts 10:45, NIV.
22. Jennings, *Acts*, 113. Original italics.
23. Burrus, "Gospel of Luke," 147.
24. Jennings, *Acts*, 110.
25. See Wa Thiong'o, *Decolonising the Mind*; Mbembe, *On the Postcolony*; Tetteh, *Inspired African Mystical Gospel*, 25; Giliomee, "Making of the Apartheid Plan," 383–84; Fanon, *Wretched of the Earth*, 6; Mignolo, "Delinking," 463–64; Vellem, "Un-Thinking the West."

Just as God's identity is decolonized, so does God's decolonized personhood open the possibilities of alternative consciousness. Godself participates in transgressing the colonial myth. In that case, it is no leap to propose that the faithful, having committed to decolonizing the mind, should also participate in God's transgressive actions. From this interpretation, it is plausible and imperative to bring "to the foreground other epistemologies, other principles of knowledge and understanding and, consequently, other economies, other politics, other ethics."[26]

Moving the Center for Hermeneutics

> But [the literature of struggle] did point out the possibility of moving the center from its location in Europe towards a pluralism of centers; themselves being equally legitimate locations of the human imagination. —Ngũgĩ wa Thiong'o[27]

My contemplation of the postcolonial understanding of centrality has brought us to the possibility of a movement that unveils a universal center and moves towards a plurality of centers. The following points came to the fore concerning unveiling a universal center within colonial history: 1) The European center was considered universal. 2) This center was represented by maleness and whiteness.[28] 3) The European center, as the center of the empire, promoted itself through violence as universal truth and the only legitimate perspective to view the world.[29] 4) There was a close relationship between the European center and the Christian faith.[30] 5) The European center misrepresented the other.[31]

Regarding the movement of a plurality of centers, the following came to the fore: 1) A myriad of centers of knowledge can exist as "legitimate locations of the human imagination."[32] 2) Mutual circulation of knowledge and ideas between the various centers is encouraged.[33] 3) Hermeneutic

---

26. Mignolo, "Delinking," 453.
27. Wa Thiong'o, *Moving the Centre*, 26.
28. See Cornell and Seely, *Spirit of Revolution*, 123.
29. See Wa Thiong'o, *Moving the Centre*; Mbembe, *On the Postcolony*; Ellis, "South Africa."
30. See Ellis, "South Africa."
31. See Wa Thiong'o, *Moving the Centre*, 37.
32. Wa Thiong'o, *Moving the Centre*, 26.
33. See Wa Thiong'o, *Moving the Centre*, 40, 47.

questions related to each center should be asked regarding perspective, motives, and interests.

Unveiling the Universalized Center of Interpretation

> The historical-critical method employed by biblical studies largely depends on the study of words. But the work of biblical scholars is principally confined to dry and technical details and is written as if the study of words has no contemporary or ethical consequences. Most of their work is driven by religious motive and confessional interest, and as such there is a failure to note the varied colonial contexts which provided the language for biblical texts. —RASIAH SUGIRTHARAJAH[34]

From Sugirtharajah's observation, one could argue that an ingrained blindspot of the historical-critical method lies in an assumption of normativity as if no center of hermeneutics is involved. Instead, as with all epistemological and hermeneutic endeavors, one's center influences knowing and understanding. But the postcolonial insights have proposed the potential that one should honestly, as far as possible, try to name one's center[35] while simultaneously relating to other centers of perspective.[36] Indeed, this understanding of centers and the relationality between and amongst them is difficult, but we could also imagine the newness entering such a dialogue.

As Sugirtharajah correctly proposes about the historical-critical method of hermeneutics, an inherent flaw lies in the "religious motive[s] and confessional interest[s]," which are upheld by the colonial language of the historical context within the text.[37] Thus, without explicitly noting the pervasiveness of colonial discourse, interpreting the text as, let's say, *Reformed* or *intellectual* will merely reiterate the dominant forms of a colonial-centered knowledge system. And thus, the call to move the center:

> Decentering of dominant forms of knowledge which envisioned the world from a single privileged point of view which simultaneously elevated the cultures of the colonizer—religions, arts,

---

34. Sugirtharajah, *Exploring Postcolonial Biblical Criticism*, 23–24.
35. Vellem, "Un-Thinking the West," 1.
36. Mignolo, "Delinking," 459.
37. Sugirtharajah, *Exploring Postcolonial Biblical Criticism*, 23–24.

dances, rituals, history, geography—and undermined those of the colonized.[38]

Returning to Acts 10, in his 1994 commentary, Charles Barret proposes that one decisive and clear element is present in the text, "the expansion of Christianity into the non-Jewish world."[39] He goes on to show that the understanding that God does not show favoritism indicates that "non-Jews are welcomed into the people of God." The implication is that Peter, as the "chief actor," is the one who welcomes these gentiles. Barret makes an interesting proposition by claiming that Peter is the one who is converted in the text; however, his conversion merely includes other bodies into the epistemological center from whence he comes. Thus, in this line of thought, although Peter is *converted*, he does not need to take seriously the alternative center Cornelius represents and contributes to. However, it is not that Barret understands Cornelius to represent an alternative center.

In Barret's interpretation of the person of Cornelius, he focuses on Cornelius' closeness to the synagogue, his fear of God, and his piety:[40]

> That [Cornelius] had faith is proved by the fact that he prayed, which no one does unless he believes. . . . What Luke means is that God judges men fairly in accordance with their opportunities. Cornelius is not to be condemned for not believing a Gospel he had never heard; he is rather to be rewarded for having lived up to the opportunities he had had by being allowed to learn more and to believe more. God looks with favor upon those who so far as they know him fear him, and so far as they know what righteousness is practice it.[41]

In this line of thought, Cornelius becomes merely an extension of the normative Jewish cult. His perspective is and becomes more legitimate to be accepted by God the closer he can get to the Jewish center. Furthermore, this becomes the only reason God, through Peter, includes this gentile: Cornelius is already centered in the Jewish perspective, or at least as close as possible.[42] This interpretation leaves no room for surprise or the unexpected. There is only one universally acceptable and legitimate center where God can show mercy.

38. Sugirtharajah, *Exploring Postcolonial Biblical Criticism*, 15–16.
39. Barret, *Acts 1–14*, 495.
40. Barret, *Acts 1–14*, 497–98.
41. Barret, *Acts 1–14*, 498.
42. Also see Pelikan, *Acts*, 132.

Postcolonial Homiletics?

Moving to a Plurality of Centers

> This moment schools us in divine transgression. God brings Peter to one outside of the covenant, transgressing God's own established boundary and border. —Willie Jennings[43]

In Jennings' interpretation of Acts 10, any center which claims superiority or universalism is denied. Even the idea that Godself can stand as some sort of normative and correct location of truth is moved toward other possibilities. Godself becomes legitimate from different perspectives because God transgresses boundaries and borders established by Godself.

Concerning Peter, Jennings claims that Peter does not grasp the depths of what he is saying when he claims that God does not show favoritism. "What matters is that [Peter] has been driven to this place by sheer divine desire and not his own desire."[44] The change of speech Peter undergoes, and the actions leading him to Cornelius are by no means a standard extension of the Jewish cult. It is something new, unexpected, and unanticipated. Jennings continues with the following about Peter:

> Peter is at the threshold of revelation. That revelation is not of God's wider palette for people but that Peter's range of whom to love and desire must expand until it stretches beyond his own limits into God's life. God is pressing Peter's aesthetic toward death and resurrection—the dying and rising to new desires is now the call emerging for him. This revelation, however, is beyond Peter. God, at this moment, is pressing him to his limits.[45]

In this line of thought, Peter's understanding of what God is doing is beyond his epistemological and lingual center. Peter is unable to fathom or name this movement to new possibilities. Jennings, unfortunately, does not contemplate the location of culture and perspective of Cornelius. William Willimon makes two critical observations. Firstly, he takes seriously the fact that Cornelius is a gentile to his very core, falling before Peter to worship him. Secondly, the third space of negotiation is created in the house of Cornelius.[46] Cornelius is not a blank canvas on whom another center of perspective can be written. He comes as he is. At the same time, this

---

43. Jennings, *Acts*, 110.
44. Jennings, *Acts*, 110.
45. Jennings, *Acts*, 111–12.
46. Willimon, *Acts*, 97.

contested space expects a conversion or change of center by both Peter and Cornelius.[47] Thus, this space is the third possibility, neither that of Peter nor Cornelius, but the newness that enters their interaction. Furthermore, the Gospel is preached from Peter's and Cornelius' locations in this contested space.[48] Moreover, Cornelius' inclusion into the church does not take place in an attempt or rule to become like Peter; it takes place within the gift of heteroglossia from the Holy Spirit as the alienation of the normative center where newness breaks through.[49]

At this junction of space and identity, I turn to postcolonial identity.

Postcolonial Identity and Hermeneutics

> Cultural globality is figured in the *in-between* spaces of double-frames: its historical originality marked by a cognitive obscurity; its decentred [and fragmented] "subject" signified in the nervous temporality of the transitional, or the emergent provisionality of the "present."—HOMI BHABHA[50]

Our contemplation on postcolonial identity has brought forth three potential avenues of rethinking identity. 1) the relationship between identity and time; 2) the concept of hybridity; 3) the body as an important marker of identity.

My discernment has determined that the colonial gaze has arrested the relationship between identity and time. This means that the West-centered perspective has delimited *the other* within fixed categories such as savage, unsophisticated, and backward.[51] When, however, *the other* co-opts the Western perspective, they (merely in a proxy manner) are integrated and conceived as human by the stalwarts of the Western perspective.[52] Furthermore, Black Theology of Liberation failed to transcend this colonial gaze fixed in time even as it sought to liberate those oppressed by colonization. Finally, postcolonial thought's understanding of the importance of time and space unlocks the possibility of identity as decentered and fragmented.[53]

---

47. Willimon, *Acts*, 96.
48. Willimon, *Acts*, 98–99.
49. See Burrus, "Gospel of Luke," 147–48.
50. Bhabha, *Location of Culture*, 216.
51. See Drichel, "Time of Hybridity"; Cornell and Seely, *Spirit of Revolution*, 123.
52. See Wa Thiong'o, *Moving the Centre*, 34.
53. See Bhabha, *Location of Culture*, 217.

At the limits of time and space, I placed a hybrid identity on the table as an alternative c/enter to the fixed center of the Western gaze.[54] However, hybridity enters the world by disrupting the spatial realities of fixedness.[55] Thus, hybridity is the convergence of space and time beyond colonial fixedness and is always contingent. This is the third space where stereotypes are dislodged, and freedom exists to negotiate identity. Finally, the postcolonial identity, as an internal feature, must underscore human agency. The agency of postcolonial identity comes to the fore in mimicry, improvisation, and creativity.[56]

The Decentered and Fragmented Identity: Peter, Cornelius, and God

> Representation is one of the major rhetorical devices by which colonial ideology exercises its power. . . . Colonial caricatures generate two types of representation. One is the misrepresentation of the colonized, and the other is the affirmative presentation of the colonizer. —RASIAH SUGIRTHARAJAH[57]

Returning thus to Acts 10, I will look at how the text interpreters portray the three principal characters: Peter, Cornelius, and God. Once more, I attempt to closely read time, space, and agency within the text. Taking postcolonial identity seriously is one of "[i]nterrogating colonial and contemporary practices of representation of the 'other' and the power relations that lie behind the production of such knowledge."[58] Thus, this endeavor is one of understanding identity and, inevitably, power relations.

Earlier in this chapter, I opined that Grosheide understood the identity of Peter as a gatekeeper and normative conduit for the gospel to the gentiles. In this understanding of Peter, Peter's identity is stuck in time and stereotyped. His identity when meeting with Cornelius, delivering the sermon, and being interrupted by the heteroglossia of the Holy Spirit through the gentiles does not influence or change Peter's identity as the one with the

---

54. Drichel uses c/enter to indicate that in the act of moving the center of identity towards hybridity the slash (/) is "a silent reminder . . . that this centre is decentred, both split and double," Drichel, "Time of Hybridity," 605.

55. See Bhabha, *Location of Culture*, 38

56. Lartey, *Postcolonializing God*, 216–28.

57. Sugirtharajah, *Exploring Postcolonial Biblical Criticism*, 161–62.

58. Sugirtharajah, *Exploring Postcolonial Biblical Criticism*, 15.

"bijzondere taak der apostelen."[59] From this point of view, no negotiation of identity or change in identity takes place. The fact that these gentiles have now heard the gospel is merely the expected "expansion of Christianity into the non-Jewish world."[60]

If, however, the power dynamics of the colonial normative center are questioned, and Peter's identity can be seen as negotiable, three aspects come to mind. 1) Because of the pericope of Acts 10:9–22, Peter dislodges his identity from the Jewish law, which forbids association between Jew and gentile, and he enters the home of Cornelius. 2) Peter only attempts to make theological sense of God's revelation to the gentile Cornelius. Peter's speech act is not normative but an attempt at sense-making. As Willie Jennings claims,

> This revelation, however, is beyond Peter.... Peter can only locate in these historic unprecedented actions an ethic of divine acceptance.... Peter is saying that if any Gentile does what is right and fears the Holy One, they will be acceptable to God. But there is much more going on here.[61]

Indeed, there is much more going on! The text is ambivalent. Did the gentiles come to faith because Peter preached? Or was Peter brought to this negotiation space to be interrupted so he could listen? There is no sure answer, yet the interruption of the Holy Spirit[62] and the astonishment of the Peter group[63] showcase hybridity regarding Peter's positionality. Any possibility of Peter as gatekeeper ought to be questioned. Instead, his identity is decentered and fragmented by the contested space of Cornelius' home. 3) But it is in verse 47 where Peter discloses to the greatest extent the negotiation of identity in this space: "Can anyone keep these people from being baptized with water?"[64] This rhetorical question is loaded. At stake is the very identity of the Christian person and Peter himself. As Jennings aptly claims, what happens is not merely the acceptance of the gospel but "the joining of Jew and Gentile."[65] Peter's identity has radically shifted with the

---

59. Grosheide, *Handelingen der Apostelen*, 169. "Exceptional task of the apostle" (my translation).

60. Barret, *Acts 1–14*, 495.

61. Jennings, *Acts*, 113–14.

62. Acts 10:44, NIV.

63. Acts 10:45, NIV.

64. Acts 10:47, NIV.

65. Jennings, *Acts*, 116.

proposal on Peter's lips that these gentiles have no alternative but to be baptized and the criticism which will follow for this action.[66]

I now turn to the person of Cornelius. Barret represents Cornelius as a pious person close to the Jewish cult, with a fear of God.[67] He relentlessly claims this persona as the reason why God looks with favor upon Cornelius and welcomes him into the Christian community. However, Barret seems to ignore the characteristics of Cornelius, which would contradict and disgrace the personification of Cornelius as pious. Willie Jennings, on the other hand, does not:

> [Cornelius] is a man of war, bound to the Roman state. He is a master, an owner of slaves. He is a ruler, a leader of men. He is what so many men and women in this world aspire to be and what so many peoples want to be defined as—a strong self-sufficient people who look to the world like one unified, strong, self-sufficient man. Cornelius is an aspiration, but he is also an anomaly. He is a God-fearer. He is one who stands at the door of Israel and knocks, praying the prayers of God's people as though he is one, following the gestures of worship and life of God's people as though he is one, embodying the hopes of God's people without them knowing it. Cornelius is thusly a living contradiction. He is in the old order, but his actions are preparing him for the new order.[68]

Jennings is expecting a movement from the old order to the new one, but I propose that no such expectation is necessary. The identity of Cornelius does not cease to be hybrid at the end of the narrative. Cornelius is not baptized and then ceases to be a centurion or is expected to change his career. At least, no such mention is made in the text. He is still a living contradiction!

Furthermore, how Acts 10 ends leave the question open concerning Cornelius' agency as a participant in the expansion of the Christian community. On the one hand, the narrator gives no agency to Cornelius beyond Acts 10.[69] On the other hand, in imagining Cornelius' interaction with others beyond the biblical narrative, an improvisational and creative

---

66. Acts 11:2, NIV.

67. Barret, *Acts 1–14*, 498.

68. Jennings, *Acts*, 105.

69. Sugirtharajah proposes that a denial of agency to the marginalised and poor exists within the writings of Luke. Thus, although Luke seemingly champions for those on the margins of society, they lack agency within the Lukan narratives. See Sugirtharajah, *Exploring Postcolonial Biblical Criticism*, 163.

Contemplating Postcolonial Hermeneutics

tone might best represent how he participates beyond the text. Indeed, it is speculation, yet the narrator does not have the urge to tell the reader that Cornelius had to submit to rigorous theological training under Peter to get his theology *just* right.

Lastly, the identity of God. In my reading of Grosheide, I am convinced that he only locates God's identity within the preaching of Peter. In other terms, God's identity is found in the revelation that God does not show favoritism.[70] For Grosheide, God is not active beyond what Peter says in the biblical text. However, Grosheide does not understand this revelation to Peter to be something new in the world; on the contrary, referring to Rom 10:12, all nations stand equal before God.[71] For Grosheide, there can be no identity formation, movement, or hybridity in God. His reference to Romans 10 is also problematic, for Rom 10 could only have been written because God transcended the laws which excluded *all nations* from entering the faith community. Thus, Grosheide attributes a static, a-temporal identity to God.

Similarly, Barret locates God's identity in fixedness. He correctly lays claim on the participation of God in the narrative through the angels and the Holy Spirit, yet sees God's activity as "the final critical stage in the extension of the Gospel and the expansion of the church."[72] Once more, nothing unusual takes place: no newness, surprise, or strange new world. He also claims that while the Christians opposed the gentiles' inclusion in the faith community, "God overruled their objection and himself brought the Gentiles in." That God included the gentiles is undoubtedly true. But it was not merely an overruling of the objections of the Christians which took place. Barret makes it sound as if the exclusion of the gentiles was because of the Christians' personal tastes rather than God's law. Stated otherwise, the text is not about God overruling the Christians but about God overruling Godself.[73]

It interests me why both Grosheide and Barret want to defend a fixed image of God. Why must the proposal be that God is static? What are the power dynamics behind understanding God as predetermined, inflexible,

---

70. Grosheide, *Handelingen der Apostelen*, 167.

71. Grosheide, *Handelingen der Apostelen*, 168

72. Barret, *Acts 1–14*, 491.

73. Jennings claims that Peter is not disobedient when resisting the command to kill and eat but calls the whole movement from exclusion of the unclean, to inclusion, "the birth pangs of the new order." Jennings, *Acts*, 107.

and unchangeable? Do these characteristics of God underscore the colonial myth of our world as not subject to change? Or even the possibility of questioning the way things are?

In Jennings' contribution regarding God's identity, he mentions God's action as transgressing borders and boundaries in intimate spaces where the Jew and gentile should not be together.[74] Once more, God transgresses not just any boundaries and borders but God's established ones.[75] "Divine touch is always unexpected and usually unconventional."[76] From this perspective, the agency of God moves beyond the confines of fixedness and predetermination. God brings forth a newness, unexpected, concerning how the world is.

Furthermore, this newness is facilitated within spaces of negotiation. In this line of thought, God's identity is fluid because the security of the law can be eliminated. This elimination of security brings forth the risky and arduous struggle for new relations and ways of being in the world.

And yet, one more identity must be considered; the reader of the text.

The Decentered and Fragmented Identity of the Reader

> [B]iblical interpretation has yet to integrate various historical biblical readers from different points in the Christian history of the last nineteen hundred and ninety-six years. In short, the question of how different flesh and blood readers have acted out the biblical story in history, and how their act illumines some meaning of the text needs to be integrated into academic biblical studies. —Musa Dube[77]

Although thorough consideration of the reader as interpreter and identity is outside of the scope of this study, I think it essential to take note of Dube's critique and proposal. Biblical interpretation is not restricted to academia; thus, the postcolonial endeavor should take notice of "flesh and blood readers" and how they have enacted biblical stories. There is a need for

---

74. Jennings, *Acts*, 109.
75. Jennings, *Acts*, 110.
76. Jennings, *Acts*, 111.
77. Dube, "Toward a Post-Colonial Feminist Interpretation," 12.

empirical research concerning how different people read and engage with biblical narratives in thought and praxis.[78]

Dion Forster did a critical study on the impact of the location of culture and the interpretation of forgiveness in Matt 18:15–35.[79] In the study, Forster found that the differing locations of culture brought forth differing understandings of forgiveness as portrayed in the biblical text. With regards to the first group, which partook in the reading and interpretation of the text, Forster has the following comments:

> Thus, the predominantly Black Christian grouping understood forgiveness in Matthew 18.15–35 in a collective manner. Forgiveness is understood as an expression of the restoration of social harmony in the community with clear expectations of social, economic and political transformation.[80]

When it came to the second group, predominantly white Christians, Forster concluded:

> The majority of the group tended to understand forgiveness as an individual spiritual phenomenon that was enacted between the sinning party and God. Thus, they found it difficult to identify with the pain and struggle of others (the persons sinned against) as a condition for forgiveness.[81]

However, an unusual exception took place in the second group. There was an individual who was aware of the hermeneutical influence the white perspective has on interpreting the text and recognized the responsibility of visible reconciliation within the South African social fabric. Forster suggests that this individual's ability to transcend hermeneutical constraints stems from the fact that the "participant had worked in a predominantly Black educational setting."[82]

Thus, within the lived experience of decentering and fragmentation within the space and time of secular life, this reader could interpret the biblical text from a vantage point of consideration for different centers.

---

78. I am aware of the Intercultureel Bijbellezen project in the Netherlands and contextual Bible study project of the Ujamaa Centre at UKZN, but more must still be done.

79. In the South African context where the study took place, the divide of location of culture is on the grounds of race.

80. Forster, *(Im)possibility of Forgiveness?*, 184.

81. Forster, *(Im)possibility of Forgiveness?*, 189.

82. Forster, *(Im)possibility of Forgiveness?*, 188.

Furthermore, although Forster himself does not claim this, in my reading of the quotations of this individual, I find that this participant is grappling with the relationship between the differing centers:

> I know, I know, I agree with you, I'm say [sic] we need to maybe it [sic] take it to a different level to say, "we recognize their pain and that hurt and then . . . our response needs to be different.[83]

This idea of "a different level" represents three distinct movements. One, the moment of recognition that time changes the other beyond a centered perspective; two, the importance of spaces where different others can have communal lived experiences; and three, the agency of the other to be different than oneself.

83. Forster, *(Im)possibility of Forgiveness?*, 188.

Chapter 5

Some Concluding Thoughts[1]

As the concluding chapter, I return to the South African homiletic landscape to reflect—from a postcolonial perspective—on the two most significant movements in Homiletics: prophetic preaching and aesthetic homiletics.

PROPHETIC PREACHING

In 1995 Hennie Pieterse published a research project, *Desmond Tutu's Message*, which focuses on the anti-apartheid sermons of Desmond Tutu. Herein Pieterse makes three crucial proposals that will become prominent in understanding prophetic preaching in South Africa. Firstly, Desmond Tutu's preaching steeped in Black Theology of Liberation (BTL) is "critical prophetic preaching."[2] Secondly, Tutu's prophetic sermons were underscored by a "vision for the South African society, which is . . . based on [Tutu's] Christian interpretation of the reign of God."[3] Thirdly, Tutu's sermons transcended the politics of apartheid.[4]

At the intersection of these three points, Pieterse makes the following proposal for a model for preaching in democratic South Africa:

---

1. Part of this chapter was published as an article—"On Justice and Beauty in Recent South African Homiletics: a Post-Colonial Reflection"—in *Acta Theologica* 40, suppl. 29 (2020) 176–94.

2. Pieterse, "Prophetic Preaching in Context," 96.

3. Pieterse et al., "Structure of Thought," 55.

4. Pieterse et al., "Structure of Thought," 48.

[L]iberation theology and prophetic preaching should guide the churches' contribution to the struggle for LIBERATION FROM POVERTY through reconstruction and development.[5]

This sentence represents the watershed moment when BTL is coined as prophetic preaching: "preaching which is keenly aware and takes seriously the ethical-political-societal dimensions of preaching."[6] Before this, BTL was univocally practiced from the perspective of black oppression as "a relevant gospel to the Black community."[7] In the apartheid context, BTL empowered black people, claiming God is amongst them in their struggle for freedom.[8]

However, with Pieterse's proposal, a change occurs, and newness enters the homiletic landscape. Pieterse grapples earnestly with the globalized context South Africa has engaged in since 1994. Moreover, his endeavor envisions an intersection between the insights of BTL, the potential of prophetic preaching as a vision for South Africa, and the parameters of this globalized reality. This is essentially a novum and notable contribution. Furthermore, Pieterse's study is the first instance within South African homiletic thought where BTL is considered positively. Prior, BTL was either wholly ignored[9] or vehemently opposed.[10] Internationally, during this time, a tradition of prophetic homiletics has already contemplated the ethical, political, and societal aspects of preaching.[11]

Something exciting occurs in this historical timeframe for prophetic preaching in South Africa. Not only was Pieterse the first South African theologian to consider BTL as the privileged contextual methodology for preaching, but he developed this proposal quite considerably. Three stages can be discerned. Firstly, contextual analysis of poverty in South Africa. Secondly, the relationship between the rich church and the poor church. And thirdly, critical engagement with governmental corruption.

Pieterse's 2001 book, *Preaching in a Context of Poverty*, outlines the positive sentiments of the global economic system and liberal democracy within the new South Africa. The hope for a better future in South Africa

---

5. Pieterse, "Prophetic Preaching in Context," 97.
6. Laubscher and Wessels, "Prophetic Word on Studies," 178.
7. Boesak, *Black and Reformed*, 29.
8. Mofokeng, "Black Christology," 4, 15.
9. Vorster, "Eise aan die Fereformeerde Prediking."
10. Smith, *Kansel en Politiek*, 106.
11. See Brueggemann, *Prophetic Imagination*; Harris, *Preaching Liberation*.

revolved around job creation in the public, private, and informal sectors as endeavors to curb the problem of poverty.[12] Regarding prophetic preaching, Pieterse underscores the homiletic and hermeneutic process with the caveat that the "preacher must be existentially familiar with the local context of poverty."[13]

From this point of departure, Pieterse moves to the relationship between the rich and poor churches. To be clear, Pieterse uses the terms "church *for* the poor" and "church *of* the poor."[14] In an attempt to constitute relationality between preaching, poverty, and this dualistic church, Pieterse outlines "a theory which combines prophetic preaching with diaconal community development."[15] This implies a "missionary diaconate" where the rich church aids the poor church in poverty relief in collaboration with governmental and non-governmental organizations. Although Pieterse calls for equal cooperation amongst these churches, the duality unintendedly invalidates egalitarian collaboration. Furthermore, Pieterse's prophetic preaching must inevitably lose all possibilities of imagination beyond the contextual limits and becomes a hyper-contextual ecclesiology of development and poverty relief, with sermons underscoring this agenda.

In *Preaching in a Context of Poverty*, Pieterse opines that prophetic preaching will expose all forms of power abuse that "weaken and jeopardize the position of the poor."[16] When Pieterse wrote these words, he did not mention any corrupt dealings within the government and spoke mainly in a positive tone about the administration of South Africa. However, since the presidency of Jacob Zuma (2009–18), many homiletic theologians have started contemplating prophetic preaching as preaching that exposes corruption.[17] I consider that this overwhelming contemplation on prophetic preaching was sparked by the previously mentioned understanding proposed by Pieterse regarding Tutu as an archetype for prophetic preaching. To be clear, homiletic theologians disagree on what prophetic preaching entails. Tubbs Tisdale and De Wet determined at least four visions for

---

12. Pieterse, *Preaching in a Context*, 64–68.
13. Pieterse, *Preaching in a Context*, 92.
14. Pieterse, *Preaching in a Context*, 112.
15. Pieterse, *Preaching in a Context*, 121.
16. Pieterse, *Preaching in a Context*, 90.
17. See de Wet and Kruger, "Blessed Are Those That Hunger"; Tubbs Tisdale and de Wet, "Contemporary Prophetic Preaching Theory"; Kruger and Pieterse, "Reasons Why"; Wessels, "Contemplating Allan Boesak's Fascination."

prophetic preaching in South Africa.[18] There are even more today, but the point remains, within the context of political corruption, prophetic preaching as exposing corruption becomes the perceived be-all and end-all of homiletic thought.

REFLECTING ON PROPHETIC PREACHING'S PURSUIT OF ECONOMIC JUSTICE

The endeavor of Pieterse to integrate BTL and the democratic context through prophetic preaching is remarkable. At the same time, when prophetic preaching becomes the trend of homiletic thought during corruption, thorough reflection becomes necessary. Moreover, later movements in BTL and new contemplation on postcolonial theory paint a complex picture concerning the relationship between liberation and economic globalization. Once more, prophetic preaching to pursue economic justice must be scrutinized.

In Ngũgĩ wa Thiong'o's book, *Decolonising the Mind*, he concludes that his endeavor is "a call for the rediscovery of the real language of humankind: the language of struggle."[19] In later contemplation on the insights the language of struggle brings to the table, he makes the following comment:

> But [the literature of struggle] did point out the possibility of moving the center from its location in Europe towards a pluralism of centers; themselves being equally legitimate locations of the human imagination.[20]

The point being made by Wa Thiong'o is both the necessity for speaking (and perceiving) the world from the location of struggle. Thus, there is a movement from a fixed and normative center of location (the Western center) toward a center of struggle. However, this movement does not propose a new fixed center but rather the possibility of pluralism of locations of culture from whence the world can be perceived.

Although BTL is a theology of struggle and, thus, a postcolonial theology, its hermeneutical center must be critiqued. For BTL during apartheid, the hermeneutic center is the location of culture of black people as oppressed and colonized in South Africa. In Gerald West's opinion, the

---

18. Tubbs Tisdale and De Wet, "Contemporary Prophetic Preaching Theory," 4–8.
19. Wa Thiong'o, *Decolonising the Mind*, 108.
20. Wa Thiong'o, *Moving the Centre*, 26.

marginalized, poor, and oppressed are still the interlocutors for the hermeneutics of BTL in democratic South Africa.[21] This movement of the center for BTL is essential and profound, a hermeneutical move Pieterse correctly makes.

However, from a postcolonial perspective, this movement of hermeneutical perspective proposes that the location of culture of the poor should become the new fixed and normative center. This is problematic for three reasons. First, it underscores Western epistemology, which works with the concept of a normative center excluding all other centers. Two, it undermines the existential limits of one's location of culture, proposing that anyone could ipso facto imagine and experience the location of culture of *the other*. And three, it becomes blind to subtle changes in interlocutors.

Regarding the first, a new fixed center excludes other epistemological possibilities, undermining the struggle for human liberation and privileging some locations of culture over others. Secondly, the possibility of misrepresentation enters the fray. And thirdly, as Vuyani Vellem proposes, interlocutors can change and have indeed done so for BTL in democratic South Africa towards "a black middle-class person rather than the poor non-person."[22]

Returning to prophetic preaching, all three of these critical points are also reasonable critiques of prophetic preaching. If prophetic preaching should be from the perspective of the poor, what is the relationship with other locations of culture? Secondly, is it possible, for example, for a middle-class religious leader to understand the existential experience of poverty without misrepresentation? And are the poor, in reality, the interlocutors of prophetic preaching?

Let's consider the possibility that the middle-class person is the interlocutor of prophetic preaching as preaching against corruption. This change of interlocutor influences all three points I have raised above. But first, let me interrogate the interlocutor of prophetic preaching in more detail.

The first and most obvious indication of a change in the interlocutor is the timeframe prophetic preaching became the normative conversation amongst South African homiletic theologians: at the height of governmental corruption. At the same time, the goal of prophetic preaching becomes that of exposing corruption:

---

21. West, *Stolen Bible*, 353–54.
22. Vellem, "Interlocution and Black Theology," 4.

POSTCOLONIAL HOMILETICS?

> Every preacher should discern the content of our prophetic preaching in contemporary South Africa in the specific context of the congregation. General issues that can be addressed are corruption by officials administering state funds, maladministration of state funds and unskilled people in crucial positions in the private sector who cannot do the job, but are there because they are ANC cadres due to the policies by the government to redeploy people to other positions after they are found guilty of corruption or maladministration in a previous government position.[23]

> In our view, the essence of prophetic preaching is that it proclaims the biblical message critically in a society that tends to deviate from its God-given form and destiny, in the process equipping Christians to radiate the light of the kingdom of heaven and its righteousness revealingly and energizing with a view to refocusing the world on its destiny in a restored relationship with God.[24]

> But the main issue is still how Christians and Christian leaders can start to act against corruptive practices. It is clear that it will be irresponsible if churches remain silent.[25]

I want to propose this: prophetic preaching only becomes the focal point for homiletic thought once the middle-class person's livelihood is in jeopardy because of government corruption. From this insight, *the poor* become merely the proxy interlocutor to petition for the rights and privileges of the middle class. In other words, prophetic preaching within homiletic thought only uses "an imaginary agent interlocutor in some imaginary South African township"[26] to advocate for the middle class.

The acute perceiver of the situation would realize that the positionality of the poor in the current South African context, whether corruption is prevalent or not, is a nonperson without value. To state it in the words of Vuyani Vellem,

> I wonder if there is anything moral or ethical about capitalism or neoliberal capitalism. . . . The restoration of the authority of the people means the restoration of identity-sustaining narratives and their compatible logically coherent ethical arguments with the feasibility of the planning of courses of action. It means that the victims of colonization and apartheid become in charge

---

23. Pieterse, "Prophetic Preaching," 5.
24. De Wet and Kruger, "Blessed Are Those That Hunger," 7.
25. Kruger and Pieterse, "Reasons Why," 90.
26. Maluleke and Nadar, "Alien Fraudsters," 7.

of the *terms* of economics, not just the critique of the *content* of economic justice.[27]

Thus, in prophetic preaching's pursuit of calling out corruption, the epistemological underscoring of the status quo as neoliberal capitalism and the actual interlocutor of prophetic preaching becomes a stumbling block for contemplation on justice. Under these conditions, adequate representation of the poor, the struggle for justice, and the poor as genuine interlocutors for prophetic preaching become questionable.

AESTHETIC HOMILETICS

Although prophetic preaching is overwhelming in recent homiletic thought, aesthetic homiletics is another important focal image. Johan Cilliers has by far the largest body of work on aesthetics, but Ian Nell and Cas Vos' contributions will also be contemplated.

Convergences of Aesthetic Homiletics and Prophetic Preaching

Amid prophetic preaching as dominant homiletic discourse, Johan Cilliers questions whether the term *prophetic preaching* is helpful. He reasons that how prophetic preaching is understood within homiletics reveals "a theological[ly] unsophisticated" comprehension of the art of preaching.[28] He shows that prophetic preaching merely blends political and eschatological language on the pulpit and can take place anywhere on the spectrum of political alliance.[29] Thus, certain preachers can understand their prophetic task as a challenge to the political status quo, others as the preservation of the status quo, and still others as complete silence on the status quo.

As an alternative, Cilliers reinterprets Desmond Tutu's preaching as anticipation for God's eschatological-political future through imagination, inherently relativizing the present status quo.[30] Thus, the present becomes penultimate and God's future ultimate. Themes Cilliers identifies in Tutu's sermons are 1) an inclusive rhetoric that transgresses the boundaries of the status quo; 2) an invitation into the eschatological-political future of God

---

27. Vellem and Laubscher, "Interview with Vuyani S. Vellem," 10, 12.
28. Cilliers, "Where Have All the Prophets Gone?," 373.
29. Cilliers, "Where Have All the Prophets Gone?," 374.
30. Cilliers, "Where Have All the Prophets Gone?," 378–79.

already breaking through in the present; 3) humor which underscores the penultimate nature of the present; and 4) God-images which surprise and do not adhere to preconceived motifs of God.[31]

The alternative Ian Nell places on the table in conversation with prophetic preaching is "a theodramatic paradigm."[32] This paradigm expands the conception of right knowing in preaching to include right living through participating in the drama of God in the world.[33] In this line of thought, the pastor becomes the director of the church, which is a prophetic community "by acting as a community of love and justice." When considering the type of justice he has in mind, he proposes, as per the Confession of Belhar, taking hands, embracing one another, and giving back the bicycle.[34] He coordinates these three acts with unity, reconciliation, and justice:

> [One,] to reach out with open arms and cross the many different divides between people. . . . [Two,] The preaching process should create spaces where people feel safe to bring the victims and victimizers into authentic relationships. . . . [And three,] Throughout this process [of justice in theodramatic terms, the prophetic community] become witnesses to society in general of the ways in which each and everyone can play these roles [of justice] with integrity.[35]

Divergences between Aesthetic Homiletics and Prophetic Preaching

Although aesthetic homiletic thought converses with prophetic preaching, it diverges on moralism and religious activism. Johan Cilliers has proposed that religious activism is, in essence, the postmodern development of moralism.[36] The moralist and religious activist sermon will:

---

31. Cilliers, *Space for Grace*, 31.
32. Nell, "In Search of Meaning," 571.
33. Nell, "In Search of Meaning," 572.
34. Nell, "In Search of Meaning," 574–76. Giving back the bicycle refers to restructuring of economic system to rectify past injustices such as land redistribution.
35. Nell, "In Search of Meaning," 574–76.
36. Cilliers, "Disabling God?," 4. Cilliers and Laubscher, "Interview with Prof. Johan Cilliers," 8.

Some Concluding Thoughts

> [State] what God has done [in the past] and what God will do [in the future], but more importantly: what people must do to activate God's deeds now.[37]

Cilliers' homiletic research has led him to propose the possibility that political preaching during apartheid (to sustain the status quo) and the activism of prophetic preaching are underscored by the same tendencies of moralism. Where such preaching during apartheid called for the Afrikaner nation to act morally for God's actions to be activated,[38] so does prophetic preaching for the people today.[39]

It is from these impetuses that he moved towards aesthetic homiletics:

> But, later on, as I was searching for alternatives, I started to appreciate aesthetics as a space which does not circle the wagons to form enclaves, but rather a space where creativity and playfulness are no strangers. In this regard, my German *Doktorvater*, Rudolf Bohren, played a major role, teaching me that moralism and aesthetics are in fact the exact opposite. The one clamps down, the other opens up.[40]

With this idea that aesthetic homiletics *opens up*, three focal images emerge where aesthetic homiletics diverges from prophetic preaching to bring forth newness in the world: 1) the person of the preacher; 2) the identity of God; 3) inculturation and the human spirit.

The Person of the Preacher

> Preachers are fools. Preaching fools. At the deepest level this characterization is inescapable. For preachers proclaim the foolish, disruptive gospel of the life, death, and resurrection of Jesus. . . . Just as Jesus, like a trickster, crosses boundaries, breaks taboos, and speaks disruptive words, so preaching fools interrupt the social and religious—and homiletical—status quo. —CHARLES CAMPBELL AND JOHAN CILLIERS.[41]

---

37. Cilliers, "Disabling God?," 5.
38. See Cilliers, *Uitwissing van God*.
39. See Cilliers, "Prophetic Preaching in South Africa."
40. Cilliers and Laubscher, "Interview with Prof. Johan Cilliers," 7.
41. Campbell and Cilliers, *Preaching Fools*, 153–54.

The perspective of Campbell and Cilliers brings forth an image of the preacher which transcends and hybrids the preacher. Unlike the perception of the preacher as a sage who knows God's will for society, the fool in persona and actions decenters, fools, plays, breaks open new possibilities and fragments reality. The point Campbell and Cilliers make is that playing the fool and fooling with the play (of life) breaks open forms of existing in the world which have become stagnant, be they political, socioeconomic, or religious.[42] The idea of play could be brought in close relation to Ian Nell's idea of the preacher as director in the theatrical play of God. Although Nell[43] explicitly shies away from contemplating the person of the preacher, the ideas Campbell and Cilliers place on the table could aid in the relationship between the theodrama of the past and the contextual theodrama. In the words of Campbell and Cilliers,

> In this way [the preaching fools] constantly remind us that what is needed is not a repetition of old paradigms, but a re-creation of them—not a cloning of what was, but a clowning for what could be.[44]

As such, Nell would do well to integrate into the theodramatic paradigm the importance of a persona that reminds of recreation. Furthermore, this reframing of the person of the preacher has the implications of changing the understanding of all people. Now, the identity of persons is open for negotiation. Space and time, which underlie human identity, are absorbed into the "eschatological fluidity" of the fool's gospel.[45]

Exciting empirical homiletic research was done by Ian Nell when researching a project named *Sermon of the Layperson*. In the project, five laypersons were selected to preach a sermon each. The criteria for selection was that "the preachers should be people with influence in society through their participation in public debate," with a feel for the plight of the vulnerable.[46] This project fundamentally plays with the preacher's persona, allowing new voices and perspectives to be heard. In the future, it would be interesting to see what other voices, such as people without societal influence, would bring to the table. Furthermore, in conversation with

---

42. Campbell and Cilliers, *Preaching Fools*, 163.
43. Nell, "In Search of Meaning," 573.
44. Campbell and Cilliers, *Preaching Fools*, 163.
45. Campbell and Cilliers, *Preaching Fools*, 168.
46. Nell, "'Preaching from the Pews,'" 3.

Campbell and Cilliers, the pulpit's space becomes negotiable regarding allowing bodies previously excluded from the pulpit because of race, class, gender, sexual orientation, or any other bodily attribute.[47]

The Identity of God

In Johan Cilliers' contemplation on the Belhar Confession, he understands God's weakness, brokenness, and vulnerability from the fourth article. For Cilliers, the words "in a world full of injustice and enmity . . . God is in a special way the God of the destitute, the poor and the wronged" speak of God's choice of becoming (and being) poor, marginalized, and wronged.[48] From this perspective, contemplation on the identity of God as weak opens both the possibilities of how God is feeble and how broken people relate to God. The images Cilliers proposes as vulnerable God are, for example, God as a quadriplegic in a sip-puff wheelchair, a crucified donkey, a victim of a xenophobic attack, and a man with AIDS.[49] In the vulnerability and brokenness of God, there is a certain ugliness, about which Cilliers has the following to say:

> Beauty, understood in theological-aesthetical sense, is not annihilated by the ugly and horrific. On the contrary, the beauty of God is often revealed exactly under such circumstances: the ugliness of the cross is the strange "beauty" of God, *par excellence*.[50]

Furthermore, these contemplations on the vulnerability of God are truly contemplations on the vulnerability of humans. For Cilliers, aesthetics is locating God's activity within the lived experience of human beings, including suffering and struggle.[51]

When it comes to the God of the dance, Cilliers integrates bodily movement, dancing as anticipation for harmony, and the trinitarian perichoresis:

> But this glorious godly choreography—this is the wonder of grace—does not remain locked up in the Trinity. . . . The circular dance is thus opened up, in that God as Creator, Saviour and

---

47. Campbell and Cilliers, *Preaching Fools*, 156–57.
48. Cilliers, "Clown before the Powers," 16.
49. Cilliers, "Clown before the Powers," 17; Cilliers, *Dancing with Deity*, 169.
50. Cilliers, *Dancing with Deity*, 63.
51. Cilliers, *Dancing with Deity*, 146.

Consummator, as it were, opens up God's arms for all of creation to come and join in the joy, to come and dance with God.[52]

In this vision of God as dancing, Cilliers breaks the boundaries between God and human, body and soul, mundane and beautiful. The aesthetic imagination of dance blurs the lines between the sacred and secular, between embracing the O/other and being embraced by the O/other, and between the included and the excluded:

> A liturgy that participates in the dance of the trinity has open arms: it embraces those who have been marginalized, stereotyped, or stigmatized by society; it welcomes Aids sufferers and homosexually orientated people; it receives the poor, the powerless, the vulnerable and the voiceless.[53]

Lastly, Cilliers contemplates the absence of God. In his thoughts on space and how the event of preaching becomes "a space for grace" both as a gift when "God enters, transcends and fluidizes our spaces," and as the creation of preaching,[54] he considers the possibility of God's absence in spaces. He considers the lived experience underscored by Samuel Beckett's *Waiting for Godot* and Ben Williken's *Last Supper*, where the table is empty.[55] In the interaction between these interlocutors, Cilliers proposes the possibility that God can be a combination of absent, hidden, and elusive, one as well as another. Still, whereas Beckett's play is a tragedy of waiting, Williken's painting brings forth a *"hermeneutics of expectation."*[56] The point Cilliers makes is that God's absence makes it possible for newness to enter the world. The expectation for what is to come at the empty table opens spaces for a new understanding of faith, God, each other, the Holy Supper, and life. At the same time, the empty table speaks of the presence of the absent one through the Holy Spirit.[57] There is thus both the absence of God and the presence, the expectation of the one to come who is already there:

> This table waits upon the arrival not of Godot, who never comes.
> This table waits upon the arrival of God, who has already come.[58]

---

52. Cilliers, *Dancing with Deity*, 122.
53. Cilliers, *Dancing with Deity*, 175.
54. Cilliers, *Space for Grace*, 31.
55. Cilliers, *Space for Grace*, 42–45.
56. Cilliers, *Space for Grace*, 43.
57. Cilliers, *Space for Grace*, 44.
58. Cilliers, *Space for Grace*, 44.

Some Concluding Thoughts

Inculturation and the Human Spirit

A third important image in aesthetic homiletics is inculturation. In Cas Vos' contribution to aesthetic homiletics, he proposes a myriad of possible usages of secular poetry, novels, art, songs, theater, and films within the sermon to open the dialogue between sacred and lived experience.[59] Inevitably, Vos calls for the inculturation of the event of preaching as a critical reciprocity between cult and culture. Although he is somewhat restrained in his inculturation, underscoring the need for responsible virtue ethics for the church, his point of the possibility of Christianity overcoming the barriers between religious and lived experience through aesthetics is critical.

In a sense, Johan Cilliers' aesthetic work is inherently inculturation. His insights into visual art particularly underscore the close association between preaching, aesthetics, and inculturation. In one of his contemplations of a painting of Willie Bester, *Township Plight*, Cilliers shows acutely how the lived experience of oppression flows through myriad forms of aesthetic expression within the struggle for justice.[60] And over against the destructive heritage of the apartheid past in South Africa—symbolized by inadequate houses, a gun and bullets, and fearful faces—Cilliers finds the "triumph of the human spirit, the (colorful) transcendence of the raw realities of the South African history of Apartheid."[61] This idea of the human spirit, which triumphs over injustice, envisions newness entering the world. No, in fact, it is newness already entering the world. Yet, this newness is the encultured expression of human struggle towards transcending the unjust.

Reflecting on Aesthetic Homiletics

I am convinced that aesthetic homiletics[62] showcases strong postcolonial tendencies. Although there does not seem to be a direct influence of postcolonial thought on aesthetic homiletics, there are two points where aesthetic homiletics corresponds strongly with post-colonial theory: 1) decolonizing the mind, and 2) identity as decentered and fragmented.

---

59. Vos, "Literêr-Estetiese Benadering," 5–7.
60. Cilliers, "Just Preaching," 32–33.
61. Cilliers, "Just Preaching," 33.
62. It should be noted that Johan Cilliers and Cas Vos were influenced by Henning Luther and the likes in their aesthetic homiletics. This brings forth the interesting possibility that focal images in postcolonial thought is alive and well in what is deemed by some as colonial and European epistemology.

In the convergence between aesthetic homiletics and prophetic preaching, aesthetic homiletics questions the overarching myth of prophetic preaching, thus deconstructing it. Furthermore, aesthetic homiletics places alternatives to the restricted understanding of justice as neoliberal democratic participation on the table. Insights from thinkers throughout many disciplines, worldviews, and locations of culture are considered, breaking open new possibilities for thinking and living as the potential of decolonization of the mind.

In the endeavor of aesthetic homiletics, as I have shown, the identities of the preacher and God are decentered and fragmented in a myriad of ways. This hybridity of identity opens new spaces, pregnant with the possibility for new relationships and interpretations of the person's agency. One could, however, argue that even greater contemplation could be brought to the table regarding the agency of those most removed from societal influence. In other words, although the identity of the preacher and that of God have undergone thorough reflection, the character of the poor and vulnerable seems to be still fixed in time and space. Further contemplation of inculturation may be able to dislodge this rigid identity.

Postcolonial Homiletics?

When I endeavored this project, I was intrigued by the potential of postcolonial thought as a conversation partner for homiletics. The timeframe coincided with the Fallist movements in South Africa and abroad. I expected to find what could be considered an utterly anti-Western sentiment in postcolonial writings. Such a sentiment certainly exists but is not the overwhelming direction of thought this book has brought forth.

Instead, my threefold conceptual framework, in its simplicity of decolonizing the mind, moving the center, and creating a postcolonial identity, have opened avenues to a much more diverse, complex, and even contentious conversation for decolonization. This is a good development for the crucial conversations around the curricula of theological education, the place of Christianity after colonization, and the culture wars at large. But most importantly, theological formation in the space and moment of the worship service.

This book, in its essence, is the hope that preaching would be concretely and contextually located within the empirical reality of the world without being overpowered by ideologies that require mental gymnastics

Some Concluding Thoughts

for the context to fit the theory. It is the dream that preaching could inspire people to live within the confines of their limited confines but to their full potential. This book is the idea that preaching could propose the best way for people to live, in their inequality, discrepancies, differences, and diversity—namely, cooperation, in all its complications, potential, and dangers.

Bibliography

Alfaro, Luis, and Pablo Lejarreta, dirs. *Money Heist: The Phenomenon*. Vancouver Media, 2020. https://www.netflix.com/title/81098822.

Barret, Charles K. *Acts 1–14*. International Critical Commentary. Edinburgh: T. & T. Clark, 1994.

Barth, Karl. *Homiletics*. Louisville: Westminster John Knox, 1991.

Bhabha, Homi K. *The Location of Culture*. London: Routledge, 1994.

Bhengu, Cebelihle. "ANC Lekgotla Outcomes in Six Quotes: 'SOEs Must Serve the People.'" *Times Live*, January 23, 2020. https://www.timeslive.co.za/politics/2020-01-23-anc-lekgotla-outcomes-in-six-quotes-soes-must-serve-the-people/.

Biko, Steve B. *Write What I Like*. Oxford: Heinemann, 1987.

Boesak, Allan A. *Black and Reformed: Apartheid, Liberation and the Calvinist Tradition*. Braamfontein, South Africa: Skotaville, 1984.

———. *Dare We Speak of Hope? Searching for a Language of Life in Faith and Politics*. Grand Rapids, MI: Eerdmans, 2014.

———. *Kairos, Crisis, and Global Apartheid: The Challenge to Prophetic Resistance*. New York: Palgrave Macmillan, 2015.

———. "'A Hope Unprepared to Accept Things as They Are': Engaging John De Gruchy's Challenges for 'Theology at the Edge.'" *Nederduitse Gereformeerde Teologiese Tydskrif* 55 (2014) 1055–74.

———. *Running with Horses: Reflections of an Accidental Politician*. Cape Town, South Africa: Joho, 2009.

———. "Subversive Piety: The Reradicalization of Desmond Tutu." In *Radical Reconciliation: Beyond Political Pietism and Christian Quietism*, edited by Allan Aubrey Boesak and Curtiss Paul DeYoung, 131–49. New York: Orbis, 2012.

———. *The Tenderness of Conscience: African Renaissance and the Spirituality of Politics*. Stellenbosch, South Africa: Sun, 2005.

Bosch, David J. *Transforming Mission: Paradigm Shifts in Theology of Mission*. 20th Anniversary edition. New York: Orbis, 2011.

Bowers du Toit, Nadine. "Decolonising Development? Re-Claiming Biko and a Black Theology of Liberation within the Context of Faith Based Organisations in South Africa." *Missionalia* 46 (2018) 24–35.

Brueggemann, Walter. "Patriotism for Citizens of the Penultimate Superpower." *Dialog: A Journal of Theology* 42 (2003) 336–43.

———. *The Prophetic Imagination*. Philadelphia: Fortress, 1978.

———. *The Word Militant: Preaching a Decentering Word*. Minneapolis: Fortress, 2007.

Bibliography

Burrus, Virginia. "The Gospel of Luke and the Acts of the Apostles." In *A Postcolonial Commentary on the New Testament Writings*, edited by Fernando F. Segovia and Rasiah S. Sugirtharajah, 133–55. London: T. & T. Clark, 2007.

Cabrita, Joel. "Texts, Authority, and Community in the South African 'Ibandla LamaNazaretha' (Church of the Nazaretha), 1910–1976." *Journal of Religion in Africa* 40 (2010) 60–95.

Campbell, Charles L., and Johan H. Cilliers. *Preaching Fools: The Gospel as a Rhetoric of Folly*. Waco, TX: Baylor University Press, 2012.

Carvalhaes, Claudio. "Liturgy and Postcolonialism: An Introduction." In *Liturgy in Postcolonial Perspectives: Only One Is Holy*, edited by Claudio Carvalhaes, 1–20. London: Palgrave Macmillan, 2015.

Césaire, Aimé. *Discourse on Colonialism*. New York: Monthly Review, 1972.

Chirume, Joseph. "Nelson Mandela University Protest Ends—Institution Can Reopen." *News24*, March 8, 2019. https://www.news24.com/News24/nelson-mandela-university-protest-ends-institution-can-reopen-20190308.

Cilliers, Johan. "The Clown before the Powers: A South African Response to Charles Campbell's Comic Vision on Preaching." *Homiletic* 33 (2008) 11–18.

———. "Clowning on the Pulpit? Contours of a Comic Vision on Preaching." *Scriptura* 101 (2009) 189–97.

———. *Dancing with Deity: Re-Imagining the Beauty of Worship*. Wellington: Bible Media, 2012.

———. *Die Uitwissing van God Op die Kansel: Onstellende Bevindingse Oor Suid-Afrikaanse Prediking*. Cape Town, South Africa: Lux Verbi, 1996.

———. "Disabling God in an Able World? Analysis of a South African Sermon." *Nederduitse Gereformeerde Teologiese Tydskrif* 53 (2012) 1–12.

———. *God for Us? An Analysis and Assessment of Dutch Reformed Preaching during the Apartheid Years*. Stellenbosch, South Africa: Sun, 2006.

———. "Just Preaching . . . in Times of Transition: South African Perspectives." *International Journal of Homiletics* 1 (2016) 21–33.

———. *The Living Voice of the Gospel*. Stellenbosch, South Africa: Sun, 2004.

———. "Preaching as Reframing of Perspective." *In Luce Verbi* 44 (2010) 85–97.

———. "Preaching between Assimilation and Separation: Perspectives on Church and State in South African Society." Homiletics Seminar for Danish Pastors held in Copenhagen, June 19–20, 2008.

———. "Prophetic Preaching in South Africa: Exploring Some Spaces of Tension." *Nederduitse Gereformeerde Teologiese Tydskrif* 54 (2013) 1–15.

———. *A Space for Grace: Towards an Aesthetics of Preaching*. Stellenbosch, South Africa: Sun Media, 2016.

———. "Where Have All the Prophets Gone? Perspectives on Political Preaching." *Stellenbosch Theological Journal* 1 (2015) 367–83.

———. "Worshipping in the Townships: A Case Study for Liminal Liturgy?" *Journal of Theology for Southern Africa* 132 (2008) 72–85.

Cilliers, Johan, and Cas Wepener. "In Herinnering aan die Kinders . . . Wat aan Honger en Koue Moet Sterf: Liturgie in 'N Konteks van Armoede." *Nederduitse Gereformeerde Teologiese Tydskrif* 45 (2004) 364–72.

Cilliers, Johan, and Martin Laubscher. "Interview with Prof. Johan Cilliers." *Acta Theologica* 38 (2018) 5–14.

"The Confession of Belhar." https://kerkargief.co.za/doks/bely/CF_Belhar.pdf.

Bibliography

Copeland, M. Shawn. *Enfleshing Freedom*. Minneapolis: Fortress, 2010.

Cornell, Drucilla, and Stephen D. Seely. *The Spirit of Revolution: Beyond the Dead Ends of Man*. Cambridge: Polity, 2016.

Cornille, Catherine. "Empathy and Otherness in Interreligious Dialogue." In *Dynamics of Difference: Christianity and Alterity*, edited by Ulrich Schmiedel and James Matarazzo, 221–29. London: Bloomsbury, 2015.

Costas, Orlando. E. "Evangelism and the Gospel of Salvation." *International Review of Mission* 63 (1974) 24–37.

Cox, Harvey. *The Secular City: Secularization and Urbanization in Theological Perspective*. 2nd ed. Princeton, NJ: Princeton University Press, 2013.

De Gruchy, John W. "Christian Humanism, Progressive Christianity and Social Transformation." *Journal for the Study of Religion* 31 (2018) 54–69.

———. "Is It Possible for a White South African Male to Enter the Kingdom of Heaven?" The 8th Steve de Gruchy Memorial Lecture, Cape Town, 2019.

De Oliveira Andreotti, Vanessa, et al. "Mapping Interpretations of Decolonization in the Context of Higher Education." *Decolonization: Indigeneity, Education & Society* 4 (2015) 21–40.

Denny, Lindie, and Cas Wepener. "The Spirit and the Meal as a Model for Charismatic Worship: A Practical-Theological Exploration." *HTS Theological Studies* 69 (2013) 1–9.

De Wet, Fritz W. "Naming and Nurturing Reality from a Heart Renewed by Grace." *HTS Theological Studies* 71 (2015) 1–8.

De Wet, Fritz W., and Ferdi P. Kruger. "Blessed Are Those That Hunger and Thirst for Righteousness: Sharpening the Ethical Dimension of Prophetic Preaching in a Context of Corruption." *Verbum et Ecclesia* 34 (2013) 1–10.

Dolamo, R. T. H. "Does Black Theology Have a Role to Play in the Democratic South Africa?" *Acta Theologica*, suppl. 24 (2016) 43–61.

Drichel, Simone. "The Time of Hybridity." *Philosophy and Social Criticism* 34 (2008) 587–615.

Dube, Musa. W. "Toward a Post-Colonial Feminist Interpretation of the Bible." *Semeia* 78 (1997) 11–26.

Dwane, Sigqibo. "Gospel and Culture." *Journal of Black Theology in South Africa* 1 (1987) 18–25.

Eiesland, Nancy L. *The Disabled God: Towards a Liberatory Theology of Disability*. Nashville: Abingdon, 1994.

Ellis, S. D. K. "South Africa and the Decolonization of the Mind." Inaugural lecture: Vrije Universiteit Amsterdam Desmond Tutu Chair, Amsterdam, 2009.

Fanon, Frantz. *The Wretched of the Earth*. 2nd ed. New York: Grove, 2004.

Finfind. "The SA SMME COVID-19 Impact Report." November 2020. https://www.banking.org.za/wp-content/uploads/2021/05/SA-SMME-COVID-19-Impact-Report.pdf.

Forster, Dion. *The (Im)Possibility of Forgiveness? An Empirical Intercultural Bible Reading of Matthew 18:15–35*. Stellenbosch, South Africa: Sun Media, 2017.

Foucault, Michel. "The Order of Discourse." In *Untying the Text: A Post-Structuralist Reader*, edited by Robert Young, 51–78. Boston: Routledge & Kegan Paul, 1981.

Giliomee, Herman. "The Making of the Apartheid Plan, 1929–1948." *Journal of South African Studies* 29 (2003) 373–92.

Bibliography

Goba, Bonganjalo. "Toward a Quest for Christian Identity: A Third World Perspective." *Journal of Black Theology in South Africa* 2 (1988) 31–36.

Gregory, Brad. S. *The Unintended Reformation: How a Religious Revolution Secularized Society*. Cambridge: The Belknap, 2012.

Grosheide, Frederik W. *De Handelingen Der Apostelen: Eerste Deel*. Korte Verklaring Der Heilige Schrift. Edited by G. Aalders et al. Kampen, The Neth.: J. H. Kok N. V., 1941.

Haidt, Jonathan. "Why the Past 10 Years of American Life Have Been Uniquely Stupid: It's Not Just a Phase." *The Atlantic*, April 11, 2022. https://www.theatlantic.com/magazine/archive/2022/05/social-media-democracy-trust-babel/629369/.

Harris, James. H. *Preaching Liberation*. Minneapolis: Fortress, 1995.

Hook, Derek. *(Post)Apartheid Conditions: Psychoanalysis and Social Formation*. New York: Palgrave Macmillan, 2013.

Hurrell, Max. "ZOL." *YouTube*, May 1, 2020. https://www.youtube.com/watch?v=jE2l2qXwtiU.

Jeffery, Anthea. "Critical Race Theory & Race-Based Policy: A Threat to Liberal Democracy." *@Liberty*, May 2021. https://irr.org.za/reports/atLiberty/liberty-critical-race-theory-race-based-policy-a-threat-to-liberal-democracy.

Jennings, Willie J. *Acts*. Belief: A Theological Commentary on the Bible. Louisville: Westminster John Knox, 2017.

Jiménez, Pablo. "Towards a Postcolonial Homiletic: Justo L. González's Contribution to Hispanic Preaching." In *Hispanic Christian Thought at the Dawn of the Twenty-First Century: Apuntes in Honor of Justo L. Gonzále*, edited by Alvin Padilla et al., 159–67. Nashville: Abingdon, 2005.

Jordaan, Roxanne. "The Emergence of Black Feminist Theology in South Africa." *Journal of Black Theology in South Africa* 1 (1987) 42–46.

Katongole, Emmanuel. *Born from Lament: The Theology and Politics of Hope in Africa*. Grand Rapids, MI: Eerdmans, 2017.

Kaunda, Chammah. J. "The Denial of African Agency: A Decolonial Theological Turn." *Black Theology* 13 (2015) 73–92.

Kearney, Richard, and Liam Kavanagh. "An Interview with Richard Kearney: 'Facing God.'" *Journal of Philosophy & Scripture* 1 (2004) 1–10.

Khabela, M. Gideon. "The Socio-Cultural Dynamics of the Struggle for Liberation and the Coherence of Black Faith." *Journal of Black Theology in South Africa* 3 (1989) 23–38.

The Kiffness. "Max Hurrell—ZOL (Unofficial Music Video by the Kiffness)." *YouTube*, May 8, 2020. https://www.youtube.com/watch?v=UshEeyv8YZM&ab_channel=TheKiffness.

Kruger, Ferdie P., and Hendrik J. C. Pieterse. "Reasons Why Government Leaders, Officials and Church Leaders Have to Act against Corruption." In *Corruption in South Africa's Liberal Democratic Context: Equipping Christian Leaders and Communities for Their Role in Countering Corruption*, edited by Ferdi Kruger and Ben De Klerk, 64–95. Durbanville, South Africa: AOSIS, 2016.

Lamola, J. M. "Towards a Black Church: A Historical Investigation of the African Independent Churches as a Model." *Journal of Black Theology in South Africa* 2 (1988) 5–14.

Lamola, Malesela J. "The Thought of Steve Biko as the Historico-Philosophical Base of South African Black Theology." *Journal of Black Theology in South Africa* 3 (1989) 1–13.

Bibliography

Lartey, Emmanuel Y. *Postcolonializing God: An African Practical Theology*. London: SCM, 2013.

Laubscher, Martin. "Belhar, Liturgy and Life?" *Studia Historiae Ecclesiasticae* 45 (2019) 1–20.

Laubscher, Martin, and Wessel Wessels. "A Prophetic Word on Studies in Prophetic Preaching? Re-Visioning Prophetic Preaching's (Post)Apartheid Condition." In *Theology and the (Post)Apartheid Condition: Genealogies and Future Directions*, edited by Rian Venter, 171–87. Bloemfontein, South Africa: Sun Media, 2016.

Leander, Hans. "With Homi Bhabha at the Jerusalem City Gates: A Postcolonial Reading of the 'Triumphant' Entry (Mark 11.1–11)." *Journal for the Study of the New Testament* 32 (2010) 309–35.

Lutheran World Federation. "Chicago Statement on Worship and Culture: Baptism and Rites of Life Passage." *Studia Liturgica* 28 (1998) 244–52.

Lutheran World Federation's Study Team on Worship and Culture. "Nairobi Statement on Worship and Culture." https://worship.calvin.edu/resources/resource-library/nairobi-statement-on-worship-and-culture-full-text.

Maimela, Simon S. "Current Themes and Emphases in Black Theology." In *The Unquestionable Right to Be Free: Black Theology from South Africa*, by Itumeleng J. Mosala and Buti J. Tlhagale, 101–12. Johannesburg: Skotaville, 1986.

———. "Faith That Does Justice." *Journal of Black Theology in South Africa* 3 (1989) 1–14.

———. "Theological Dilemmas and Options for the Black Church." *Journal of Black Theology in South Africa* 2 (1988) 15–25.

———. "What Do the Churches Want and Expect from Religious Education in Schools?" *Journal of Black Theology in South Africa* 1 (1987) 43–49.

Makinana, Andisiwe. "Parliament Gives Go-Ahead for Land Expropriation without Compensation." *Times Live*, December 4, 2018. https://www.timeslive.co.za/politics/2018-12-04-parliament-gives-go-ahead-for-land-expropriation-without-compensation/.

Maluleke, Tinyiko S. "Black and African Theology after Apartheid and after the Cold War: An Emerging Paradigm." *Exchange* 29 (2000) 193–212.

———. "Black and African Theologies in the New World Order: A Time to Drink from Our Own Wells." *Journal of Black Theology in South Africa* 96 (1996) 3–19.

———. "Christ in Africa: The Influence of Multi-Culturity on the Experience of Christ." *Journal of Black Theology in South Africa* 8 (1994) 49–64.

———. "The Crucified Reflected in Africa's Cross-Bearers." *Mission Studies* 17 (2000) 82–96.

Maluleke, Tinyiko S., and Sarojini Nadar. "Alien Fraudsters in the White Academy: Agency in Gendered Colour." *Journal of Black Theology in South Africa* 120 (2004) 5–17.

Manala, Matsobane J. "'A Better Life for All': A Reality or a Pipe-Dream? A Black Theology Intervention in Conditions of Poor Service Delivery in the Democratic South Africa." *Scriptura* 105 (2010) 519–31.

Maphanga, C. "Protest to 'Reclaim' Clifton Beach with Ancestral Cleansing Ceremony." *News24*, December 28, 2018. https://www.news24.com/News24/protest-to-reclaim-clifton-beach-with-ancestral-cleansing-ceremony-20181228.

Mashaba, Herman. "Black Lives Need to Matter Closer to Home." *The People's Dialogue*, June 7, 2020. https://www.politicsweb.co.za/politics/black-lives-need-to-matter-closer-to-home--herman-.

Bibliography

Mashele, Prince. "Ramaphosa Bankrupting State as Did JZ Before Him." *Sowetan Live*, December 2, 2019. https://www.sowetanlive.co.za/opinion/columnists/2019-12-02-ramaphosa-bankrupting-state-as-did-jz-before-him/.

Matthee, F. J. Nicolaas. "Cyber Cemeteries as a Challenge to Traditional Reformed Thanatological Liturgical Praxis." PhD diss., University of Pretoria, 2018. https://repository.up.ac.za/handle/2263/70670.

Mbembe, Achille. *On the Postcolony*. Berkeley, CA: University of California Press, 2001.

McKaiser, Eusebius. *Run Racist Run: Journeys into the Heart of Racism*. Johannesburg: Bookstorm, 2016.

Meyers, Ruth A. *Missional Worship, Worshipful Mission: Gathering as God's People, Going Out in God's Name*. Grand Rapids, MI: Eerdmans, 2014.

Mignolo, Walter D. "Delinking: The Rhetoric of Modernity, the Logic of Coloniality and the Grammar of De-Coloniality." *Cultural Studies* 21 (2007) 449–514.

———. "The Many Faces of Cosmo-Polis: Border Thinking and Critical Cosmopolitanism." *Public Culture* 12 (2000) 721–48.

Mofokeng, Mokete. "The Belhar Confession and Liturgy: A Hymnological Study." MA thesis, University of Pretoria, 2017. https://repository.up.ac.za/handle/2263/63034.

Mofokeng, Takatso A. "Black Christians, the Bible and Liberation." *Journal of Black Theology in South Africa* 2 (1988) 34–42.

———. "A Black Christology: A New Beginning." *Journal of Black Theology in South Africa* 1 (1987) 1–17.

———. "The Cross in the Search for True Humanity: Theological Challenges Facing South Africa." *Journal of Black Theology in South Africa* 3 (1989) 38–51.

———. "Following the Trail of Suffering: Black Theological Perspectives, Past and Present." *Journal of Black Theology in South Africa* 1 (1987) 21–34.

Moila, Moeahabo P. "The Role of Christ in Jon Sobrino's Liberation Theology: Its Significance for Black Theology in South Africa." *Journal of Black Theology in South Africa* 3 (1989) 15–22.

Molobi, Victor S. "The Past and Future of Black Theology in South Africa: In Discussion with Maimela." *Studia Historiae Ecclesiasticae* 36, suppl. (2010) 25–48.

Molobi, Victor S., and Willem Saayman. "A Time for Complementarity: African Theology, Black Theology and the AICs." *Missionalia* 34 (2006) 324–37.

Moltmann, Jürgen. *The Coming of God: Christian Eschatology*. London: SCM, 1996.

Mosala, Itumeleng J. "Black Theology in South Africa and North America: Prospects for the Future; Building of Alliances." *Journal of Black Theology in South Africa* 1 (1987) 35–41.

———. "Christianity and Socialism: Appropriating Moses and Jesus for National Liberation in Azania." *Journal of Black Theology in South Africa* 3 (1989) 28–37.

———. "The Implications of the Text of Esther for African Women's Struggle for Liberation in South Africa." *Journal of Black Theology in South Africa* 2 (1988) 3–9.

Mosala, Itumeleng J., and Buti J. Tlhagale, eds. *The Unquestionable Right to Be Free: Black Theology from South Africa*. Johannesburg: Skotaville, 1986.

Motlhabi, Mokgethi B. G. "Black Resistance to Apartheid." *Journal of Black Theology in South Africa* 1 (1987) 3–12.

———. "The Historical Origins of Black Theology." In *The Unquestionable Right to Be Free: Black Theology from South Africa*, by Itumeleng J. Mosala and Buti J. Tlhagale, 37–56. Johannesburg: Skotaville, 1986.

Bibliography

Muzorewa, Gwinyai H. "African Liberation Theology." *Journal of Black Theology in South Africa* 3 (1989) 52–70.

Myers, Jacob D. *Preaching Must Die! Troubling Homiletic Theology*. Minneapolis: Fortress, 2017.

Naidoo, Marilyn. "Overcoming Alienation in Africanising Theological Education." *HTS Theological Studies* 72 (2016) 1–8.

Ndlovu-Gatsheni, Sabelo J. "Coloniality of Power in Development Studies and the Impact of Global Imperial Designs on Africa." *Australasian Review of African Studies* 33 (2012) 48–73.

———. *Epistemic Freedom in Africa: Deprovincialization and Decolonization*. London: Routledge, 2018.

Neder, Adam. *Theology as a Way of Life: On Teaching and Learning the Christian Faith*. Grand Rapids, MI: Baker Academic, 2019.

Nell, Ian. "In Search of Meaning: Moving from the Prophet's Voice to Prophecy in Community: A South African Perspective." *Scriptura* 102 (2009) 562–78.

———. "Preaching and Performance: Theo-Dramatic Paradoxes in a South African Sermon." *Stellenbosch Theological Journal* 3 (2017) 309–26.

———. "'Preaching from the Pews': A Case Study in Vulnerable Theological Leadership." *Verbum et Ecclesia* 36 (2015) 1–10.

Newzroom Afrika. "No Alcohol and Tobacco Sales during Level 4 of the National Lockdown." *YouTube*, April 29, 2020. https://www.youtube.com/watch?v=nDstZ7qMIgY.

Ngcokovane, Cecil M. "Ethical Problems, Options and Strategies Facing the Black Church Today." *Journal of Black Theology in South Africa* 2 (1988) 26–33.

Ngoepe, Karabo. "ANC Will Rule until Jesus Comes, Zuma Says Again." *News24*, July 5, 2016. https://www.news24.com/News24/anc-will-rule-until-jesus-comes-zuma-says-again-20160705.

Orsmond, E., et al. *Woord en Fees: Advent 2019 Tot Koninkrykstyd 2020*. Stellenbosch, South Africa: Communitas, 2019.

Osmer, Richard R. *Practical Theology: An Introduction*. Grand Rapids, MI: Eerdmans, 2008.

Pauw, Jacques. *The President's Keepers: Hose Keeping Zuma in Power and Out of Prison*. Cape Town, South Africa: Tafelberg, 2017.

Pelikan, Jaroslav. *Acts*. Brazos Theological Commentary on the Bible. Grand Rapids, MI: Baker, 2005.

Pieterse, Hendrik J. C. "Communicative Rationality and Hermeneutical Insights for Preaching in a Context of Poverty." *Nederduitse Gereformeerde Teologiese Tydskrif* 43 (2002) 555–62.

———, ed. *Desmond Tutu's Message: A Qualitative Analysis*. Kampen, The Neth.: Kok Pharos, 1995.

———. *Preaching in a Context of Poverty*. Pretoria, South Africa: Unisa, 2001.

———. "Prophetic Preaching in Context." In *Desmond Tutu's Message: A Qualitative Analysis*, 96–111. Kampen, The Neth.: Kok Pharos, 1995.

———. "Prophetic Preaching in the Contemporary Context of South Africa." *In Luce Verbi* 47 (2013) 1–6.

Pieterse, Hendrik J. C., et al. "Structure of Thought." In *Desmond Tutu's Message: A Qualitative Analysis*, 37–55. Kampen, The Neth.: Kok Pharos, 1995.

Piketty, Thomas. *Capital in the Twenty-First Century*. Cambridge: Belknap, 2014.

Bibliography

Pillay, Jerry. "Faith and Reality: The Role and Contributions of the Ecumenical Church to the Realities and Development of South Africa Since the Advent of Democracy in 1994." *HTS Theological Studies* 73 (2017) 1–7.

Pina, Álex, creat. "Money Heist (La Casa De Papel)." Netflix. Vancouver Media, 2017–21. https://www.netflix.com/title/80192098?source=imdb.

Pitjeng, Refilwe. "'When People Zol': Dlamini-Zuma's Words Light Up Inspiration for Song." *Eyewitness News*, May 15, 2020. https://ewn.co.za/2020/05/15/nkosazana-dlamini-zuma-s-zol-utterances-light-up-inspiration-for-song.

Pui-lan, Kwok. "Postcolonial Preaching in Intercultural Contexts." *Homiletic* 40 (2015) 8–21.

Punt, Jeremy. "Postcolonial Biblical Criticism in South Africa: Some Mind and Road Mapping." *Neotestamentica* 37 (2003) 58–84.

Ramose, M. B. "The Two Hands of God in South Africa: A Review of Albert Nolan's God in South Africa." *Journal of Black Theology in South Africa* 2 (1988) 18–42.

Rossouw, Johan. "Nagmaal Is Nie Sommer Net Enige Ritueel Nie." *Netwerk24*, March 25, 2020. https://www.netwerk24.com/netwerk24/Stemme/Aktueel/nagmaal-is-nie-sommer-net-enige-ritueel-nie-20200324.

Rukundwa, Lazare S. "Postcolonial Theory as a Hermeneutical Tool for Biblical Reading." *HTS Theological Studies* 64 (2008) 339–51.

Said, Edward. *Culture and Imperialism*. New York: Vintage, 1994.

Senn, Frank. C. *The People's Work: A Social History of the Liturgy*. Minneapolis: Fortress, 2010.

Sizwe, Mnyama. "The Christian's Political Responsibility: Or the Christian Attitude to the State." *Journal of Black Theology in South Africa* 2 (1988) 48–52.

Sloan, Nate. "Constructing Cab Calloway: Publicity, Race, and Performance in 1930s Harlem Jazz." *The Journal of Musicology* 36 (2019) 370–400.

Smit, Dirk J. "Oor die Teologiese Inhoud van die Belydenis van Belhar." *Acta Theologica* 32 (2012) 184–202.

Smith, James K. A. *Desiring the Kingdom: Orship, Worldview, and Cultural Formation*. Grand Rapids, MI: Baker Academic, 2009.

———. *Imagining the Kingdom: How Worship Works*. Grand Rapids, MI: Baker Academic, 2013.

Smith, Thys. *Kansel en Politiek: 'N Evaluering van die Eietydse Preekgestaltes van die Politieke Toelogie*. Kaapstad, South Africa: Lux Verbi, 1987.

Spivak, Gayatri. C. "Can the Subaltern Speak?" In *Marxism and the Interpretation of Culture*, edited by Cary Nelson and Lawrence Grossberg, 271–313. London: Macmillan Education, 1988.

Staff Writer. "State of Disaster Faces Mounting Legal Challenges." *Business Tech*, February 16, 2023. https://businesstech.co.za/news/government/665453/state-of-disaster-faces-mounting-legal-challenges/.

Statistics South Africa. *General Household Survey*. Pretoria, South Africa: Statistics South Africa, 2014.

Steenwyk, Carrie, and John D. Witvliet. *The Worship Sourcebook*. 2nd ed. Grand Rapids, MI: Calvin Institute of Christian Worship, 2016.

Steyn, Melissa, and Don Foster. "Repertoires for Talking White: Resistant Whiteness in Post-Apartheid South Africa." *Ethnic and Racial Studies* 31 (2008) 25–51.

Bibliography

Stockwell, Clinton. "Fundamentalisms and the Shalom of God: An Analysis of Contemporary Expressions of Fundamentalism in Christianity, Judaism and Islam." *Evangelical Review of Theology* 363 (2012) 266–79.

Sugirtharajah, Rasiah S. *Exploring Postcolonial Biblical Criticism: History, Method, Practice*. Chichester, UK: Wiley-Blackwell, 2012.

Tetteh, Ishmael N. O. *The Fountain of Life: A Course in Metaphysics*. Accra, Ghn.: Etherean Mission, 1999.

———. *The Inspired African Mystical Gospel*. Accra, Ghn.: Etherean Mission, 2001.

TikTok Africa Official. "ZOL Challenge TikTok | When People ZOL They Put Saliva on the Paper | ZOL Max Hurrell." *YouTube*, May 15, 2020. https://www.youtube.com/watch?v=lIR_FUNoFXQ.

Travis, Sarah. *Decolonizing Preaching: The Pulpit as Postcolonial Space*. Eugene, OR: Cascade, 2014.

Tubbs Tisdale, Leonora, and Fritz W de Wet. "Contemporary Prophetic Preaching Theory in the United States of America and South Africa: A Comparative Studythrough the Lens of Shared Reformation Roots." *HTS Theological Studies* 70 (2014) 1–9.

Tutu, Desmond. *God Is Not a Christian: And Other Provocations*. New York: HarperCollins, 2011.

Urbaniak, Jakub. "Between the Christ of Deep Incarnation and the African Jesus of Tinyiko Maluleke: An Improvised Dialogue." *Modern Theology* 34 (2018) 177–205.

Valle, Lis. "Toward Postcolonial Liturgical Preaching: Drawing on the Pre-Columbian Caribbean Religion of the Tainos." *Homiletic* 40 (2015) 29–38.

Vellem, Vuyani. "Cracking the Eurocentric Code a Battle on the Banks of the 'New Blood Rivers.'" *Missionalia* 46 (2018) 267–87.

———. "Interlocution and Black Theology of Liberation in the 21st Century: A Reflection." *Studia Historiae Ecclesiasticae* 38 (2012) 1–9.

———. "The Symbol of Liberation in South African Public Life: A Black Theological Perspective." PhD diss., University of Pretoria, 2007. https://repository.up.ac.za/handle/2263/28958.

———. "Unshackling the Church." *HTS Theological Studies* 71 (2015) 1–6.

———. "Un-Thinking the West: The Spirit of Doing Black Theology of Liberation in Decolonial Times." *HTS Theological Studies* 73 (2017) 1–9.

Vellem, Vuyani, and Martin Laubscher. "Interview with Vuyani S. Vellem." *Acta Theologica* 38 (2018) 1–14.

Venter, Rian, ed. *Theology and the (Post)Apartheid Condition: Genealogies and Future Directions*. Bloemfontein, South Africa: Sun Media, 2016.

Volf, Miroslav. "Living with the 'Other.'" *Journal of Ecumenical Studies* 39 (2002) 8–25.

Vorster, J. M. "Die Eise aan die Gereformeerde Prediking in die Teenswoordige Kultuur van Verandering." *In Luce Verbi* 26 (1992) 451–63.

Vos, Cas J. A. "Drivers for the Writing of a Sermon about Reconciliation." *Verbum et Ecclesia* 26 (2005) 293–307.

———. "'N Literêr-Estetiese Benadering van Homiletiek in 'N Veranderende Kultuur." *In Luce Verbi* 48 (2014) 1–9.

Wa Thiong'o, Ngũgĩ. *Decolonising the Mind: The Politics of Language in African Literature*. Nairobi, Ken.: East African Educational, 1986.

———. *Moving the Centre: The Struggle for Cultural Freedoms*. Nairobi, Ken.: East African Educational, 1993.

Bibliography

Wepener, Cas. *Aan Tafel Met Jesus: Leer Ken Christus Se Tafelmaniere in Lukas en Handelinge.* Wellington, NZ: Bybel-Media, 2010.

———. "Eating and Drinking: Measurements and Recipes for Social Capital." In *Bonding in Worship: A Ritual Lens on Social Capital in African Independent Churches in South Africa,* edited by Cas Wepener et al., 159–77. Leuven, Belg.: Peeters, 2019.

———. "Gay-Gesprek in die NG Kerk Is Taai Verby." *Netwerk24,* May 19, 2018. https://www.netwerk24.com/Netwerk24/gay-gesprek-in-die-ng-kerk-is-taai-verby-20180519.

———. *Kookpunt! Nadenke Oor Woede: 'N Gelowige Reaksie van 'N Ontnugterde Nasie.* Wellington, NZ: Bybelkor, 2015.

———. "Still Because of the Weakness of Some? A Descriptive Exploration of the Lord's Supper in South Africa, 1948-2002." *Verbum et Ecclesia* 26 (2005) 614–40.

Wepener, Cas, and Hendrik J. C. Pieterse. "Angry Preaching: A Grounded Theory Analysis from South Africa." *International Journal of Public Theology* 12 (2018) 401–15.

Wepener, Cas, and Mirella Klomp. "D(i)e Verhouding Prediking, Mus(z)iek en Liturgie." *HTS Theological Studies* 71 (2015) 1–9.

Wepener, Cas, and Nicolaas Matthee. "Kubernagmaal in Virustyd." *Netwerk24,* March 18, 2020. https://www.netwerk24.com/Stemme/Menings/kubernagmaal-in-virustyd-20200317.

Wepener, Cas, et al. "The Tradition of Practical Theology at the University of Pretoria." *Verbum et Ecclesia* 38 (2017) 133–55.

Wessels, Wessel. "Contemplating Allan Boesak's Fascination with Preaching 'Truth to Power.'" *Acta Theologica* 37 (2017) 188–206.

———. "Preaching in South Africa Today: Contemplating the Contributions of Allan Aubrey Boesak." MDiv thesis, University of the Free State, 2014.

———. "Prophetic Preaching's (Post)Apartheid Condition: Genealogies and Future Directions?" Master's thesis, University of the Free State, 2016.

West, Gerald O. *The Stolen Bible: From Tool of Imperialism to African Icon.* Boston: Brill, 2016.

Willimon, William H. *Acts.* Interpretation: A Bible Commentary for Teaching and Preaching. Louisville: Westminster John Knox, 2010.

Wilson, Paul S. "General Editor's Preface." In *The New Interpreter's Handbook of Preaching,* edited by Paul S. Wilson, xxv–xxvii. Nashville: Abingdon, 2008.

www.ingramcontent.com/pod-product-compliance
Lightning Source LLC
Chambersburg PA
CBHW071457150426
43191CB00008B/1379